D0282823

# The Organization
# of American States
## *and the*
# Hemisphere Crisis

# The Organization
## of American States
### *and the*
## Hemisphere Crisis

by JOHN C. DREIER

*Published for the*
Council on Foreign Relations
*by*
Harper & Row, Publishers
*New York and Evanston*

To

*L. R. D.*

# Policy Books of the Council on Foreign Relations

With the publication of this volume the Council on Foreign Relations continues its new series of short books on important issues of U.S. foreign policy. The purpose of the series is twofold: first, to provide readers in this country and elsewhere with analytical studies of the highest quality on questions of world significance; and, second, to contribute to constructive thinking on American policies for the future. These volumes seek brevity and clarity without over-simplification, presenting the reasoned conclusions of authors with first-hand experience and special qualifications.

The Council was fortunate in persuading John C. Dreier, who served with distinction for ten years as United States Representative on the Council of the Organization of American States and has an intimate knowledge of inter-American affairs, to undertake the writing of this book. In the course of its preparation Ambassador Dreier had the benefit of the advice and comments of a special group invited to review and discuss the manuscript. The Council wishes to thank the following, who were members of that group, for giving their time and their counsel: Edward G. Miller, Jr. (Chairman),

Margaret Ball, John C. Campbell, Emilio G. Collado, Henry F. de Vries, Leland M. Goodrich, Charles C. Griffin, Walter Howe, Robert H. Lounsbury, Stacy May, John N. Plank, Walter J. Sedwitz, James H. Stebbins, and Arthur P. Whitaker. John C. Campbell, who is in charge of the series of short policy studies, edited the book and steered it to completion.

Responsibility for the statements of fact and opinion rests with the author, not with the group or the Council. The Council takes responsibility for the decision to publish the book as a contribution to thought on a subject of great moment: the future of the Inter-American System.

# Preface

The purpose of this small volume is to paint in broad outlines the main features of the Inter-American System and the Organization of American States, to indicate the principal achievements and shortcomings of the O.A.S. and to suggest the problems and opportunities that lie before it in the years ahead. This book is based primarily on the author's active participation in the affairs of the O.A.S. as a representative of the United States over a period of more than fifteen years, rather than upon extensive new research. It does not, therefore, pretend to be a comprehensive, let alone exhaustive, study of this unique international agency and the international system of which it forms a part. It is, rather, an effort to describe and to analyze the main issues on which the future of the system depends, and which are therefore of the greatest significance to the United States.

The present time is both an opportune moment and a difficult one in which to write a book on this subject. On the one hand, the O.A.S. is under public scrutiny and discussion throughout the hemisphere as perhaps never before in its history. A great public interest has been generated by the immensity of the problems facing the inter-American community and the significant role that the O.A.S. must inevitably play. On the other hand, for much the same reason, an author is hard put to relate his information and views to the rapid changes taking place upon the hemisphere scene and to escape being already outdated by the time his text reaches publication. Conscious of this fact, I have chosen the termination of the Eighth Meeting of Consultation of Ministers of Foreign Affairs, held at Punta del Este, Uruguay, from January 22 to 31, 1962, as the appropriate time to cut off this discussion.

The author is grateful to the Council on Foreign Relations for the opportunity of writing this book under its sponsorship, and to the School of Advanced International Studies for its support in the undertaking. Special thanks go to Philip E. Mosely, with whom the idea of the book was first discussed, and to John C. Campbell, who assisted ably and generously with regard to both practical and substantive problems in the course of its preparation. Invaluable suggestions were obtained from the members of the review group organized by the Council and presided over by Edward G. Miller, Jr. I am also indebted for their comments to Edward A. Jamison and Simon N. Wilson of the Department of State and to my colleague, Philip B. Taylor, Jr. While the criticisms and suggestions advanced by the aforementioned persons were helpful in many ways, the author, of course, assumes full responsibility for the statements made and views expressed in the book.

One more word to those in Latin America or elsewhere with whom I have been associated in the affairs of the O.A.S. If at some points in this volume I have written with a certain candor that does not accord with the façade of diplomatic pronouncements, it is without any intention of abusing a freedom from official responsibility. Rather it is because I sincerely believe that the frank expression of opinions is essential to human contact and understanding; that shibboleths must be exposed before realities can be perceived; and that such an approach will truly contribute to a closer friendship and mutual appreciation between the people of the United States and those of Latin America, for whom I have a deep affection and esteem.

JOHN C. DREIER

*Washington, D. C.*
*February 1, 1962*

# Contents

The Organization
of American States
*and the*
Hemisphere Crisis

# I

# The Challenge of Today

A new world is emerging in Latin America. Under the impact of twentieth-century industrialization and mass communication, deep and historic forces, long quiescent, have gradually been set in motion in this area of twenty countries comprising more than 200 million people. Like seismic disturbances that range in intensity from minor tremors to disastrous earthquakes, the forces of social and economic change in Latin America have had varying manifestations. Everywhere they have cracked the foundations of the traditional society. Here and there, breaking to the surface in volcanic outbursts, they have toppled the entire structure of political and social institutions.

This process of social revolution has affected not only the fundamental nature of Latin American institutions. It has also struck at the foundations of inter-American relations and therefore at the basic assumptions of United States foreign policy. It has called for a broad and penetrating review of our policy objectives, strategy, and tactics in the Latin American area. And inevitably it brings under the spotlight of public consideration the role and performance of the Organization of American States.

Despite the enormity of the changes that Latin America has been undergoing, the United States for long remained oblivious to them, or at best failed to sense their significance. To be sure, during recent years voices were raised to decry what was called a neglect of Latin America. However, too often such complaints interpreted neglect in terms of the relatively small amounts of economic assistance that the United States extended to its twenty neighbor republics as compared to other regions of the world. It was implicit in such criticisms of U.S. policy that the problems of inter-American relations, dimly perceived and inadequately understood, could be corrected by more generous loans and grants. The real neglect of Latin America, however, as many of our friends south of the border have vainly sought to make us realize, was in sympathy and understanding—in short, in human comprehension of what was going on in the hearts and minds of millions of Latin American neighbors. Nor can the responsibility for such neglect be placed on government alone: it was shared by all sectors of our national life, including educational institutions, news media, business groups, as well as the general public.

This widespread indifference was momentarily disturbed in the early 1950s, when Communists managed to acquire a dominating influence over the government of Guatemala. However, the successful counterrevolution led by Colonel Castillo Armas with U.S. backing lulled us once more into a brief and false sense of security. Then came the shocking treatment accorded Vice President Nixon in Lima and Caracas. But we were still unprepared for the greatest blow of all: the Cuban revolution, which turned the full force of its violence against the United States and the policies and purposes to which we attach first importance in our hemisphere relations. The present state of those relations tests the capacity of the United States to maintain its position of leadership not only in this hemisphere but also in the world-wide coalition of nations dedicated to the cultivation of human liberty.

Relations with the Latin American countries have long involved U.S. interests of the highest order. Early in our history we recognized that the security of the United States was intimately linked with the independence of the countries that emerged from the former Spanish and Portuguese empires. The Monroe Doctrine and the Treaty of

Rio de Janeiro, two outstanding innovations in American foreign policy more than a century apart, reflect this deep and continuing concern with the security and independence of the entire Western Hemisphere. Trade was likewise an important link with Latin America in the early days of the republic. Our economic interests have grown and flourished since that time to the point where economic interdependence in the hemisphere is at an all-time high. Both in trade and investment, Latin America ranks with Canada and Western Europe in importance to us. And finally, as a group of countries which have traditionally declared their allegiance to the principles of Western civilization and the concept of a world system based upon law and agreement rather than conquest, the Latin American states have constituted a powerful bloc of support in the United Nations and in other world forums where the issues of Communist imperialism versus the free world have been drawn.

In pursuit of its basic interests the United States evolved a policy toward Latin America that was in many ways remarkable. It was manifested in the development of the Inter-American System. Over a period of several decades the United States, as it grew in stature as a world power, agreed voluntarily to impose limitations on the exercise of this power with respect to its Latin American neighbors. Gradually the unilateral decision and action of the United States gave way to the sharing with the Latin American countries of responsibility for both decision and action in important areas of inter-American affairs, particularly in the maintenance of peace and security.

Yet apparently this policy, however praiseworthy in concept, has not in practice produced the results that we desired and hoped for. In the past few years, our basic interests have been challenged in Latin America as never before. The sad fiasco of the invasion of Cuba by U.S.-backed anti-Castro forces in April of 1961 marked a low point in the erosion on U.S. prestige with effects far beyond the hemisphere. Opinions hostile toward the United States are voiced loudly in the other American republics, restating antagonisms of a half-century ago. This country is again being depicted by many

Latin American intellectuals as the embodiment of an evil capitalist imperialism. The democratic people of the United States are charged with having supported dictatorships in Latin countries. We have been accused of selfishness and of disregard for the human aspirations of Latin America's multitudes despite our earnest efforts to share our power with them and extend to them economic assistance on a scale previously unmatched. The fact that many such criticisms are based upon ignorance, or distorted versions of the truth, or that they are frequently fomented by Communists and other enemies of peace and international cooperation does not diminish the significance of their existence or the seriousness of their impact.

Not that political popularity has any value in itself. Too often we have tended in foreign relations to mistake the façade of popularity for the substance of political power. While it is pleasant to be well liked, it is more important to be respected for what one really is. And it is from a lack of respect that the United States has increasingly suffered in Latin America during recent years. The results have been serious for our basic national interests in that area.

Already an unprecedented threat has developed to our security. The influence of communism and of the Soviet Union in Cuba is unquestioned, and threatens to extend itself to other countries by a marriage with the revolutionary appeal of *Fidelismo*. It would be foolish to exaggerate the present threat to the United States from Cuba's adherence to the Soviet bloc. President Kennedy has pointed out that the United States can take care of itself, and that the threat of Soviet intervention in Cuba is a far greater menace to the freedom and independence of the other Latin American countries. Yet the possibility that other Latin nations may fall into the grip of Soviet power in itself gravely undermines the foundations on which our security in this hemisphere rests.

Meanwhile, Latin American support of the United States in world affairs has also shown signs of weakening. In the United Nations, Cuba is to all intents and purposes a voting member of the Communist bloc. Talk of neutralism is heard in other countries which were formerly counted among our staunchest allies.

The Communist influence in Cuba and the repercussions of the Cuban revolution in other Latin American countries involve far more than a threat to the immediate interests of the United States. They constitute an open challenge by the Communist bloc to the political and economic system which we and the other American republics have espoused in the Western Hemisphere. This challenge represents an attack upon the concepts of political democracy and private economic enterprise, and an effort to supplant them with the Marxist-Leninist totalitarian system that has been imposed upon the nations now living under Communist rule. The movement of which Castro's Cuba is the spearhead thus brings to this hemisphere a direct experience of the conflict in political faiths that underlies the cold war.

The people of the United States have been deeply perplexed by these developments. It has been hard to understand why the supposedly friendly "good neighborhood" should turn out to be a community bristling with hostility. Apparently the familiar patterns of inter-American relationships, which seemed to work so well in past years, have lost much of their effectiveness. Efforts to negotiate with the Castro regime regarding the seizure of American properties and other bilateral problems, which had been amicably settled in the cases of Bolivia and Mexico, proved futile; approaches to the Cuban authorities met with either no response at all or renewed vitriolic attacks upon the United States. Appeals to other Latin American governments to take cognizance of the serious threat to the security of the entire continent as a result of the Communist penetration of Cuba produced agreement that the situation was indeed bad, but until very recently a deep reluctance to do anything about it. The Organization of American States, which only a few years ago both the President of the United States and the Secretary of State had characterized as the most effective and successful regional organization in history, was paralyzed when faced with the difficulties brought before it by the Communist triumph in Cuba. Widely expressed opinions that the United States should seek action through the O.A.S. on the Cuban problem led to repeated frustration. It was not until the Eighth Meeting of Foreign Ministers, at Punta del Este in January 1962, that positive action of any kind could be taken against Castro through the O.A.S. Even then, despite agreement on other resolutions, the unwillingness of six Latin American countries, including the three largest (Argentina, Brazil and Mexico), to agree to the exclusion of the Castro government from the Inter-American System revealed the deep differences of viewpoint that had developed and have persisted to the present time.

The problem of Cuba is, of course, of far broader significance than the chronic political upheavals that have characterized the past history of that island republic. The Castro revolution is now recognized as a particularly virulent symptom of the far-reaching political and social unrest that is found in one degree or another in all of Latin America. This is the social revolution that has now belatedly come to full flood in the "good neighborhood," and has opened up the innermost processes of political and social change in the Latin American countries to the danger of Communist penetration and aggression. To cope with this situation the United States has adopted policy changes of far-reaching importance, culminating in the "Alliance for Progress." Initially, the new attitude displayed by this country was received with widespread approval in Latin America, and for a time appeared to calm the turbulent waters of inter-American relations. It remains to be seen whether the new policies can be carried out with sufficient success and speed to overcome and reverse the deep currents of anti-Americanism that have been manifest in recent years and to re-establish a strong basis for future inter-American cooperation and understanding.

The United States faces a serious dilemma in Latin America. Over the years, this country has gradually relinquished to the organized community of the Western Hemisphere an increasing share of its capacity for decision and action. Yet, when the present critical moment arrived, the organized community appeared to be impotent. This situation naturally faces the United States with the necessity for a thorough re-examination of the international arrangements with the other American republics on which it has pinned such great hopes for the orderly and fair achievement of its national objectives. Is the Organization of American States capable of coping with the contemporary problems that beset the hemisphere? Or is it essentially a tangle of juridical inhibitions that render positive and effective action impossible? Can the apparent deficiencies in the O.A.S. be remedied to enable it to play the role we wish it to? Is a major reformation of the hemisphere system called for? Or must we consider the awful alternative of abandoning the effort of half a century of inter-American cooperation and returning to the unilateral exercise of power as the only reliable means of achieving necessary ends? These are some of the questions inevitably posed by the present state of inter-American relations.

In this book we shall explore the Inter-American System and its institutional body, the O.A.S., in an effort to clarify what it is, what it is not, and what it might be. Like many other aspects of inter-American relations, the O.A.S. is little known and less understood. Yet its capacity for effective performance, as well as its limitations as an instrument of foreign policy, must be understood if a wise decision regarding its future is to be reached. It is hoped that the discussion in the following chapters will contribute to that end.

# II

# The Forging of an Instrument

> The American States establish by this Charter the international organization that they have developed to achieve an order of peace and justice, to promote their solidarity, to strengthen their collaboration, and to defend their sovereignty, their territorial integrity and their independence.
> —from Article 1, Charter of the Organization of American States.

## *1. The O.A.S. and the New World*

Whatever other descriptive adjectives may be applied to the Organization of American States, one thing is certain: it is unique in the modern world. This particular international association of nations could only have developed in the Americas. It has grown out of the soil of the new world, shaped by the hopes, aspirations, and problems of the people who followed, geographically or historically, in the footsteps of the Pilgrim Fathers, the conquistadors, and the missionaries.

The name of the Organization of American States is a misleading clue to its character. This essentially administrative term implies that the O.A.S. is simply a bureaucracy engaged in the dull but practical activity of executing "projects" and "programs" on an intergovernmental level. The truth is that the O.A.S. is the main institutional manifestation of something much larger and more complex. That larger entity once had the more suggestive name of the Union of American Republics. Today it is usually referred to as the Inter-American System.

The Inter-American System is a conglomeration of many things. Most important of all, it is a set of principles that serve as the accepted basis of international conduct among the member states. It also incorporates certain purposes or objectives held in common by the constituent countries and a large number of treaties and other international agreements of varied juridical import. Finally, the Inter-American System comprises a group of organizations or agencies engaged in a variety of activities intended to assure the observance of the agreed principles, purposes, and treaty obligations and to help achieve the goals which the American states have set for themselves. For the sake of clarity we will in this volume use the term Inter-American System to refer to this broad complex of juridical principles, political policies, and administrative arrangements that has grown up among the American republics over the years, and apply the term O.A.S. to the principal multilateral organization through which the system operates.

It is indicative of the unique nature of the hemisphere organization that no date can be set down as that of its creation. To be sure, its present Charter bears the date of May 2, 1948. But that was largely an act of codification and restructuring rather than of creation. Pan American Day, celebrated each year on April 14, commemorates an earlier day in 1890 when there was signed in Washington, at what was called the First International American Conference, an agreement setting up the Commercial Bureau of the American Republics—the infant predecessor of the present administrative entity known as the Pan American Union. The date of April 14, 1890, therefore marks an important step in the formal development of the Inter-American System and, significantly, a step that resulted from the first positive move on the part of the United States to create a hemisphere organization. Yet much had gone on before

1890 that has vitally affected the development of this regional organization, influencing its basic character as well as its purposes and methods of operation. In the deliberations of the O.A.S. today, history—the actions, ideas, attitudes, and concepts of past years—is always present and continually exerts its influence on the functioning of the Organization.

Any international organization of independent, sovereign governments is essentially an instrument of the member states. Its powers are those, and only those, which its members give it. It follows that the O.A.S. has little capacity for independent action on its own, as is sometimes implied by calls for "action by the O.A.S." to solve pressing problems. Generally it can act only under such conditions and in such a manner as the member governments determine.

What gives life to this kind of organization are the political forces that play upon the member governments and determine their attitudes and policies with respect to the problems that come before it. This is particularly true of an international agency which, like the O.A.S., deals not merely with nonpolitical or technical matters but with the fundamental questions of national survival: the maintenance of international peace and security and the conduct of political and economic relations. The very existence of the Organization, therefore, is related directly to the deepest national purposes of the member states. It was created as a response of governments to the elemental problems of security, peace, national economy, and liberty. Its character is determined both by the form which those problems take and by the policies which the member states adopt to meet them.

The O.A.S. is related to three fundamental problems that are shared by the United States and all other countries of this hemisphere. First of these is the protection of the independence of the American states against encroachment from other parts of the world. All of the twenty-one American republics were once colonies of European countries. Almost all won their independence by revolution and established republican forms of government. All at one time or another have feared, rightly or wrongly, the reimposition of

European political control, whether by the Holy Alliance, Nazi Germany, or the Soviet-Communist bloc. The O.A.S. is first of all an expression of the conviction that in solidarity there lies strength for the common defense.

The second basic problem is the nature of the relations among the member states themselves—the intracontinental problem. It has two main phases. One concerns the prevention of armed conflict among the Latin American states, and the establishment of a system for the peaceful settlement of controversies between them. The more serious phase, however, concerns the relationship between the Latin American republics and the United States—a world power comprising about half the population, approximately 90 per cent of the wealth, and virtually all the military strength of the American community. As we shall see, this aspect of the problem, relatively unimportant when the first efforts were made to bring the states of the continent together, later on became, and continues today to be, one of the most powerful forces affecting the O.A.S.

Finally, there is a third basic problem with which the O.A.S. is concerned. That is the character of the political and social system which is to be nurtured in the states of the inter-American community. This phase of inter-American relations is today becoming more prominent and significant than ever as the twenty-one member states intensify their cooperative efforts to promote economic growth and social progress in a climate of political liberty.

All three of these problems are intimately related. However, North Americans and Latin Americans have, for readily understandable reasons, tended from time to time to attach a different measure of importance to each and have shaped their policies accordingly. Moreover, the basic approach of the United States and of Latin America to the fundamental questions of hemisphere relations has also differed in important respects. The development of the O.A.S. therefore reflects the coming together of two distinctive currents of national character and international policy, seeking to merge in the pursuit of a common purpose. This was evident in the way the United States and the Latin American countries approached the problem of their relations with the other states of the region from the very beginning.

By and large the United States, from earliest time right up to the present, has tended to place major emphasis in inter-American relations on the first problem: the protection of the American states against the rest of the world. In the early years of independence the United States was obstructed and threatened on two sides by England and Spain, and briefly also in Louisiana by France. Later the Russian Empire was seen extending its sway over Alaska and reaching its hand down the coast of the present Pacific Northwest. The War of 1812 was but a backwash of the Napoleonic wars. The young United States had reason to fear being a pawn, or an unwilling victim, in the game of power politics played by the European monarchies.

The response of the United States to this security problem was to reach an understanding with the British and to remove the French and Spanish threats by purchase of Louisiana and the peaceful cession of Florida. We then proclaimed in the Monroe Doctrine our opposition to any further colonization by European powers on the American continents. The Monroe Doctrine went even further. It openly declared that a fundamental difference existed between the American political system and that of the European monarchies and stated that any effort to extend their political system to the American continent would be considered prejudicial to our safety. Thus U.S. policy at this early date recognized that political as well as military aggression from outside the hemisphere was a danger to be reckoned with.

The United States had demonstrated a friendship and sympathy for the Latin American countries in their efforts to win their independence. However, neither in the Monroe Doctrine nor otherwise did the United States give any pledge to any other country that we would defend its territory or its independence. The doctrine was a strictly unilateral statement of our own policy, subject to no one else's interpretation and subordinate to no international obligation. We remained neutral during the wars of independence against

Spain and avoided entangling alliances with the Latin American states thereafter as strictly as, in observance of Washington's advice, we did with European countries.

The Monroe Doctrine expressed the major concern of the United States with the problem of security from extracontinental aggression. It also evidenced the tendency of the United States to adopt an independent and unilateral policy in pursuit of its security. In this sense, the Monroe Doctrine can hardly be viewed as a contribution to the foundation of the O.A.S. On the other hand it contained the seed of a powerful idea which did in fact contribute greatly to the growth of a united hemisphere. In his message of December 3, 1823, President Monroe clearly set forth the concept of the special identity of the "new world" and its distinct separation from Europe. In this the President of the United States and his advisers echoed a sentiment held widely in Latin America as well as the United States. America, it was believed, had a historic mission in civilization to achieve the aspirations of humanity for a life of peace, liberty, and justice which the prevalence of power struggles and reactionary social systems had made impossible of attainment in the "old world."

A similar concept was deeply ingrained in the thinking of Spanish American leaders, including the Liberator, Simón Bolívar. Striking off the chains of a corrupt and decadent empire, the Spanish American countries arose from three centuries of colonial rule to take their place as sovereign nations. Their first concern, like that of the United States, was to assure their political independence from Europe. However, Bolívar also called upon them to realize their destiny as a home of liberty and justice. To bring his dream into being, Bolívar convoked a congress of the Spanish American countries to meet in Panama for the purpose of drafting a treaty of confederation. Despite some reluctance on Bolívar's part, the United States was also invited, but the two representatives named by President John Quincy Adams were delayed by political bickering in Congress over their appointment and never reached the conference.

"When, a hundred centuries later, posterity searches out the origin of our public law, and remembers the pacts which consolidated its destiny, they will examine the protocols of the Isthmus with respect," declared Bolívar in his circular inviting the Spanish Americans to the Congress of Panama. The Liberator's prediction is well worth noting. For the "Treaty of Union, League and Perpetual Confederation" produced during three tropical summer weeks in 1826 foreshadows, if it does not explicitly incorporate, most of the important juridical principles that have a place in the O.A.S. today.

The Panama treaty, like the Monroe Doctrine, was directed primarily at the problem of defending the sovereignty and independence of the member states. Whereas the doctrine was a unilateral statement of the United States, the Panama pact would have bound all its parties to mutual defense. The parties to the treaty would have pledged themselves to settle all their disputes amicably and, in case of need, to refer controversies to the Assembly of the Confederation. The treaty also included an interesting provision whereby any member state that substantially changed its form of government would be excluded from the Confederation, and could rejoin only with the unanimous consent of all other members. The reason for this was the fear that monarchical elements might regain control of one of the new republics and subordinate its policy to that of Spain and the Holy Alliance. The readiness of the drafters of the 1826 treaty to foresee the danger of political subversion by an extra-continental force and to adopt a firm measure of defense against it has a special interest at this time when that very issue is being faced by the inter-American community with respect to the Communist domination of Cuba and the subordination of that country's policy to the interests of the Soviet bloc.

The period surrounding the Bolivarian efforts to establish a confederation of American states is often referred to in Latin American writings as the "amphictyonic" period.[1] This deliberate reference to

[1] See Francisco Cuevas Cancino, *Del Congreso de Panamá a la Conferencia de Caracas 1826-1954* (Caracas: Ragon, 1955); also Antonio Gómez Robledo, *Idea y Experiencia de América* (Mexico City: Fondo de Cultura Económica, 1960).

the precedent of ancient Greece is interesting. The amphictyonies, it will be recalled, were developed among the independent city states to protect a shrine in which they had a common religious interest. Here they would hold periodic religious festivals and commercial fairs. Their common responsibilities would be exercised by a council to which each city would appoint a member. This simple pattern of association among independent states fitted the needs of the Latin American countries, which at that time likewise sought to benefit from union without sacrificing individual sovereignty. But to qualify as an amphictyony, a religious element was also necessary. And this, in the Latin American context, was provided by the ideal of an America united, independent, and democratic, where the noblest aspirations of humanity would find their fullest expression. This mystique of America lay at the heart of the amphictyony, and as anyone who has participated in Pan American gatherings well knows, it persists to this day in the ritualistic ceremonies, the oratory, the idealism, and the emotional appeal which characterize so many of such meetings.

It is the particular role of Latin America to have given both to the concept and to the reality of the regional system a large portion of its idealism. Perhaps Bolívar and his contemporaries strayed from the path of practicality in projecting so grand a design for an international organization. The treaty of Panama failed of ratification, and Bolívar was disillusioned in his ideas of Spanish American confederation. But the ideal persisted, despite apparent failures, and the spirit of the Bolivarian amphictyony moves through the halls of the O.A.S. today. For the United States, in due course, also seized upon the idea of American unification, and proceeded to work out policies that resulted in the actual creation of a hemisphere organization.

## 2. *Pan Americanism and the Issue of Intervention*

To James G. Blaine, Secretary of State under two presidents, goes the major credit for the establishment of a regional organization of the Americas. Blaine, however, approached the matter in a fundamentally different manner than had Bolívar and his contemporaries. The United States in the late nineteenth century was a strong power, fully capable of defending itself. At that stage of history there was little need to associate the Latin American countries with the defense of American independence. Blaine's interest in Latin America had other purposes: the encouragement of a system of arbitration as a means of maintaining international order, and the development of closer economic relations with the Latin American states. Under Blaine's leadership, what became known as the Pan American movement was born and in turn brought forth the international organization that has grown into the present O.A.S.

The nature of the Pan American movement launched in 1889-90 is indicated by the topics discussed at the First Conference. Aside from the important subject of arbitration of international disputes, most of them dealt with commerce: adoption of uniform standards and regulations affecting trade, promotion of land and maritime transport between North and South America, and the like. And if anyone is inclined to question the continuity of history in inter-American affairs, let him note that one of the recommendations approved by the Pan American Conference in 1890 called for the establishment of an International American Bank. This idea, which did not then receive the enthusiastic support of the United States, remained an abstraction for seventy years, despite repeated attempts by Latin American governments and some U.S. officials to have such an institution set up. In 1958 the United States changed its position and agreed to the organization of the Inter-American Development Bank, which is today playing a central role in implementation of the new and vigorous cooperative effort based on the Alliance for Progress.

The embryonic international organization established in 1890 on the initiative of the United States was thus a far cry from the grandiose plan envisioned by Bolívar. It was an essentially practical proposition. It had little to do with political matters. It certainly involved no treaty obligations for mutual defense; it said nothing about the kind of political and social system that should prevail in the Americas. But establishment of the International Union of the American Republics and its secretariat, with an annual budget of $36,000, set in motion an evolutionary process that has flowered into the present O.A.S. with its broad function of maintaining peace and security and promoting the political, economic, and cultural progress of the peoples of the member states.

The most important phase of this evolutionary process was a development which, if not unforeseen, had been only vaguely intimated. Not commercial relations but political relations with the United States became the main problem for the Latin American countries in the decades following the establishment of their Commercial Bureau. At the heart of this problem, and the cause of its intensity, was Latin America's fear of the growing power of the United States. Anxieties had been sown when the United States annexed Texas and then seized a large part of the Republic of Mexico. They were nourished on such events as filibustering expeditions by Americans in Central America, and by numerous suggestions in "Yankee" governmental circles that Cuba should be incorporated into the United States. Some of Blaine's economic proposals were attacked as being dangerously like the Prussian *Zollverein* that had paved the way for the establishment of the German Empire. Then came the era of frank and deliberate military interventions in the Caribbean area under the pretext of upholding the Monroe Doctrine. Over a period of more than three decades a sharpening struggle developed over the issue of intervention. So long as this conflict remained unresolved, it virtually stultified the Pan American movement. And it left permanent scars on inter-American relations.

The position of the United States in this situation was both logical and realistic. Now virtually a world power, the United States felt secure in the Western Hemisphere between the two oceans and saw little need for any mutual defense arrangements with the other American republics. This view was reinforced by the situation in Latin America, where political instability and economic backwardness resulted in a dismal lack of effective power.

The United States, therefore, leaned heavily upon the unilateral policy of the Monroe Doctrine. Far from asking the Latin American countries to share in the responsibility for defending the hemisphere, the United States assumed to itself the responsibility for its defense against possible European intervention. It gradually took for itself the role of policeman for the entire Western Hemisphere, and at times let this be known with an arrogance that chilled the hearts of the Latin American peoples. The classic expression of this attitude was the assertion of Secretary of State Olney in 1895 that "Today the United States is practically sovereign on this continent, and its fiat is law upon the subjects to which it confines its interposition."

Having assumed the right to serve as protector of the Americas, the United States took the logical and easy step of considering itself their mentor as well. This took the form of the Roosevelt corollary to the Monroe Doctrine, under which the United States asserted the right to intervene in Latin American countries in order to prevent the intervention of European powers in circumstances of political or economic chaos. Under this policy the United States intervened in the Dominican Republic, in Haiti, and in Nicaragua. In addition, the "Colossus of the North" used its power in support of its strategic objectives in Cuba, Puerto Rico, and Panama. President Wilson employed military force to support constitutional government and U.S. interests in Mexico.

Among Latin Americans the course taken by U.S. policy created both distaste and apprehension. They felt themselves threatened with becoming virtual protectorates of the United States. Fear of the United States grew throughout Latin America, and with fear came hatred. One path—however narrow—was open to the Latin American countries in their effort to obtain from the United States a greater assurance of respect for their sovereignty and independence: the tiny, incipient international organization. The development of the Inter-American System during the years from 1890 to 1933, therefore, was dominated by efforts of the Latin American republics to secure the adoption of certain basic principles that would govern the relations among the member states of the Union, and restrain the power of the United States. Small wonder that these principles bulk so large in the present Charter of the O.A.S. and evoke so firm an allegiance on the part of the Latin American governments.

In drafting a code of law that would restrain Yankee power, the Latin American jurists invoked principles most of which had roots in the Bolivarian period: all states were juridically equal; international controversies must be settled by peaceful means; the use of force in such cases is proscribed; aliens are subjected to the same laws as citizens in each country; civilization must rest on democracy and social justice. Intense interest and much controversy centered on the principle of nonintervention. It became clear that, so long as the United States refused to accept a rule that would prohibit it from intervening under any circumstances in the internal affairs of the other American republics, there would be no peace in the Pan American family.

The reluctance of the United States to accept the princple of nonintervention was not due to any arbitrary desire to impose its will upon its sister republics. There were, in fact, as there are today, strong elements of public opinion in the United States that condemned the sending of marines to take over foreign countries, and criticized, for example, the bluster with which Theodore Roosevelt "took" the Isthmus of Panama in order to build the canal. Yet the U.S. view on intervention, although opposed by many leading Latin American jurists, had a strong basis in international law at that time. In most cases, moreover, strong reason for intervention existed: governments had ceased to exercise control; law and order had disappeared; constitutions had been violated; property had been seized without compensation; foreigners, as well as nationals, had been subject to, or threatened with, violence and denied proper protection. Charles Evans Hughes put it in succinct terms when he said: "What are we going to do when government breaks down and American citizens are in danger of their lives? Are we to stand by and see them killed because a government in circumstances which it cannot control, and for which it may not be responsible, can no longer afford reasonable protection?" [2] A problem of fundamental importance is posed here that continues to plague inter-American relations.

The issue was finally drawn at the Sixth Inter-American Conference at Havana in 1928, before which Mr. Hughes made a brilliant defense of American policy. He succeeded in having the issue postponed, but it was a Pyrrhic victory. It became clear to the United States that continuation of its intervention policy would only worsen the already badly damaged state of inter-American relations and render virtually impossible the maintenance of any useful regional association.

## 3. *Nonintervention and the Good Neighbor Policy*

Like most important changes in national and international policy, the shift by the United States from a policy of unilateral intervention to one of collective responsibility was a gradual one. The first step was to liquidate the situations which had outraged Latin American opinion. In the field of doctrine and policy, the United States, in the Clark memorandum of 1928, formally abandoned the Roosevelt corollary to the Monroe Doctrine. The military interventions in the Dominican Republic, Haiti, and Nicaragua were liquidated as rapidly as circumstances permitted. The Platt Amendment, under which the United States was given the right to intervene in Cuba, was abrogated in 1934. A new treaty regarding the canal was negotiated with Panama in 1936, eliminating some of the more objectionable aspects of the original agreement.

Finally, as the most significant landmark in this epoch-making change, the United States reversed its formal, long-standing position and at the Seventh Inter-American Conference, held in Montevideo in 1933, accepted the principle of nonintervention. Although Secretary Cordell Hull's approval of this principle was hedged by a reservation, that cloud was removed by the subsequent action of

[2] Quoted in A. V. W. and A. J. Thomas, *Non-Intervention* (Dallas: Southern Methodist University Press, 1956), p. 60.

the U.S. delegation at the Buenos Aires Conference for the Maintenance of Peace (1936) in approving, without reservation, an even stronger statement of the nonintervention principle.

The change in U.S. policy toward inter-American affairs was strongly supported by public opinion throughout the country. It was widely recognized that the older policy of unilateralism and intervention had not worked. If the purpose was to promote stable and orderly governments in other countries, the effort was a clear failure: in neither the Dominican Republic nor Haiti, nor in Nicaragua, did the American occupation produce a political system of which the American people could be proud. Nor did it help American interests of a more tangible nature: the widespread anti-Yankee sentiment provoked by the interventions could hardly pave the way for a more receptive attitude toward American investments and trade, or for that solidarity which the United States now sought as a bulwark for the defense of the hemisphere. Finally, the extension of U.S. power by force over other countries was fundamentally repugnant to American public opinion.

The subversive activities of Nazi and Fascist sympathizers during the 1930s underscored the need for a new approach to the problem of hemisphere security. Large Italian and German communities offered opportunities for the development of fifth columns dedicated to the spread of pro-Axis propaganda in the new world, and for the carrying on of espionage and sabotage. The security of the American continents required the enlistment of wide popular support for hemisphere solidarity in the Latin American countries. Only with such backing could their governments take the measures necessary to control the German and Italian agents and their local sympathizers.

## 4. Collective Security: The Treaty of Rio de Janeiro

The abandonment of unilateral intervention represented one side of the new coin of U.S. policy. The development of a system of collective responsibility for hemisphere security constituted the other. One might have expected that the Latin American republics would have responded enthusiastically to indications that the United States was prepared to move in this direction. But fear and distrust of the United States and its motives had become deeply rooted in Latin American attitudes. The process of developing an effective collective security system was slowed by the fear that any such system might be manipulated to impose the will of the United States on its weaker neighbors. The consistent observation by the United States of its nonintervention commitments, both in word and in deed, coupled with the outbreak of World War II, gradually overcame Latin American reluctance. There followed a period of intense activity in building a true international organization in the Americas, destined to play an important role in the defense of the hemisphere in World War II—an organization which in form and powers is essentially that which exists today.

The product of this period of development is largely incorporated in two basic treaties that form the foundations of the O.A.S.: the Inter-American Treaty of Reciprocal Assistance of 1947 (known as the Treaty of Rio de Janeiro) and the Charter of the Organization of American States concluded the following year. Let us trace the main features of each, starting with the development of the Treaty of Rio de Janeiro, which came first in time and established the all-important obligations on which rest the system of collective security.

Essentially the inter-American security system embraces two main concepts: consultation in case of threats to the peace; and collective action to prevent or repel aggression.

The idea of consultation in the event of threats to the peace was implicit in the Bolivarian plan for the amphictyonic association of the American republics. It owes its present position as an outstanding feature of the O.A.S. to an initiative of the United States at the Buenos Aires Conference in 1936. Two years later, at the Eighth Inter-American Conference in Lima, the consultative procedure was further developed with the adoption of a plan for personal meetings of foreign ministers. The outbreak of World War II less than a year later provided an urgent reason for putting this system of consultation into effect.

Three meetings of foreign ministers were held during World War II. They provided the mechanism for the coordination of inter-American policy with respect to the war and for the development of new and more effective means of inter-American cooperation. At Panama (1939) a hemisphere policy of neutrality was adopted, a last and futile effort to isolate the American hemisphere from the European war. When the Nazi armies overran the European continent, it was recognized that more realistic methods of dealing with the aggressor states were needed. A major step in the development of the collective security system was taken with the adoption at the Second Meeting of Foreign Ministers, held at Havana in 1940, of Resolution 14 which declared that

> . . . any attempt on the part of a non-American State against the integrity or inviolability of the territory, the sovereignty or the political independence of an American State shall be considered as an act of aggression against the States which sign this declaration.

In the event such an act of aggression were committed, or there were reason to believe that one was being planned,

> the nations signatory to the present declaration will consult among themselves in order to agree upon the measures it may be advisable to take.

The declaration of Havana thus set forth the principle of inter-American solidarity that an attack against one American state was to be considered an attack against all. The decisions of the Third Meeting of Consultation at Rio de Janeiro (1942) gave practical effect to this principle following the attack on Pearl Harbor. The principle was broadened at the Inter-American Conference on Problems of War and Peace, in Mexico (1945), by the Act of Chapultepec which virtually repeated the Havana text but with the important omission of the restrictive reference to non-American states, thus making it applicable to any form of aggression, whatever its origin.

Adopted under wartime powers of the participating governments, the formula of the Act of Chapultepec was given permanent validity in the Treaty of Rio de Janeiro, in 1947. But before this could be done, the United Nations had come into being. The founding of a new world organization occasioned, on the one hand, an intensive activity of the Latin American countries to defend the integrity of the newly developed regional security system and, on the other, the adoption of slight changes in that system to make it conform to the provisions of the United Nations Charter.

At the San Francisco Conference in 1945 the Latin American governments were determined to prevent insofar as possible the intervention of non-American powers in the maintenance of peace and security among the American states. As a result of the Chapultepec Conference they had gained a revitalized confidence in their ability to cooperate with the United States in a regional system. They therefore strongly opposed the adoption of any provisions in the United Nations Charter that might render the regional organization inoperative. Moreover, with an intense devotion to the principle of juridical equality of states, they fought against the big-power veto in the U.N. They saw, perhaps better than many others, the possibility of a deadlock in the Security Council as a result of a veto, and insisted that the ability of the regional agency to act in time of crisis should not be dependent upon the prior authorization of the Security Council.

Largely as a result of the Latin Americans' insistence on their position, the delegates drafting the United Nations Charter adopted Article 51, recognizing the right of individual and collective self-defense in case of armed attack until the Security Council of the U.N. takes the necessary measures to restore peace and security. Thus, it was reasoned, if an armed attack took place against an American state—from whatever source—the regional American system could deal with it on the basis of self-defense. A veto might prevent the Security Council from acting, but this inaction would free, rather than obstruct, the American states in taking the necessary defensive measures. This freedom, however, was limited to cases of armed attack—and did not exist with reference to other types of aggression or to threats of attack.

The Treaty of Rio de Janeiro, therefore, establishes two types of obligation. The first deals with armed attack. Drawing upon Article 51 of the United Nations Charter, it provides that in case of such attack all parties to the treaty are required to assist the attacked state immediately. The nature of this immediate assistance is left to the discretion of each party, but all are also bound to consult as soon as possible to decide upon collective measures. The decisions regarding collective measures are to be taken by a two-thirds majority.

The other type of obligation under the Rio Treaty concerns acts of aggression other than armed attacks, and all threats of aggression. In such circumstance, the parties to the treaty are bound only to consult, no prior unilateral action being either called for or authorized. Decisions of the Organ of Consultation may include the imposition of certain sanctions set forth in the treaty.[3] They range from the breaking of diplomatic and consular relations to the interruption of transportation and communications, the severance of economic relations, and the use of armed force. Decisions to take such action are binding upon all parties to the treaty, although the treaty itself realistically recognizes that no state can be required to use armed force without its consent.

In the absence of an armed attack, is the O.A.S. legally authorized to take any action involving sanctions, or does all such action require the authorization of the U.N. Security Council? The answer to this question is of great importance to the regional agency now that the Security Council is so often reduced to a state of paralysis due to the veto. The kind of aggression which the Latin American countries, no less than those in other regions, are now apt to face is of a sort that intentionally avoids an overt armed attack that would bring into play the right of self-defense recognized in Article 51 of the United Nations Charter.

[3] The generic term "Organ of Consultation" used in the treaty was later defined in the O.A.S. Charter as the Meeting of Foreign Ministers. Decisions under the Rio Treaty require a majority of two-thirds of the states entitled to vote.

Article 53 of the same Charter states that "no enforcement action shall be taken under regional arrangements or by regional agencies without the authorization of the Security Council." The key to this provision lies in the interpretation of the words "enforcement action." Do they cover any measures adopted by a regional organization to enforce its decision on a recalcitrant state, from the breaking of diplomatic relations to the use of armed force? Or do they refer only to the application of armed force? These questions were raised in a realistic way in 1954 when the United States and other American governments considered what action the projected meeting of consultation of the O.A.S. might take with respect to Guatemala, knowing full well that the Soviet Union would readily veto any move by the Security Council to authorize regional measures of a forceful character. Due to the course of events, no decision was precipitated at that time. Then the problem arose again in the O.A.S. with respect to the Dominican Republic in 1960.

At the Sixth Meeting of Consultation of Ministers of Foreign Affairs, held at San José, Costa Rica, a decision was taken to break diplomatic relations and to sever economic relations with Generalissimo Trujillo's regime, beginning with traffic in arms and implements of war—the first time the O.A.S. applied the sanctions of the Treaty of Rio de Janeiro. Although no formal decision was taken on the issue raised by Article 53 of the United Nations Charter, the matter was touched upon during the meeting. The prevailing view, implicit in the action taken against the Dominican Republic, was that in Article 53 the words "enforcement action" meant only the use of armed force, and that the severance of diplomatic and commerical relations did not require the authorization of the Security Council.

In accordance with both the United Nations Charter and the Treaty of Rio de Janeiro, full information on the measures taken by the Sixth Meeting of Consultation was sent by the O.A.S. to the Security Council. There the Soviet Representative, invoking Article 53, submitted a draft resolution under which the Council would have approved the action taken by the O.A.S. at San José. The representatives of the three American states which were members of the Council, however, submitted an alternative draft by which the Council would merely "take note" of the O.A.S. action. By adopting the American alternative rather than the Soviet proposal, and thus avoiding any formal approval or disapproval of the O.A.S. action, the Security Council in effect endorsed the view held by the Sixth Meeting of Foreign Ministers: that authorization of the Security Council was not necessary. An important precedent was thereby established.

The Treaty of Rio de Janeiro was adopted at the high tide of enthusiasm for the creation of a regional security system. For the Latin American countries it marked a high point in their confidence in the policy and purposes of the United States. For the United States the treaty amounted to the strongest obligation that it has ever contracted to assist other states in the event of armed attack. It will be noted that under the terms of this treaty the United States can be obligated to break off diplomatic relations and sever all economic relations with an aggressor state when two-thirds of the Latin American countries so decide, even if the United States may not be in agreement with that decision.

The gravity of this obligation must be weighed in the light of the realities of the voting situation. From this standpoint, there are two politically significant elements in the O.A.S.: the United States with its great military power but only one vote; and Latin America with its twenty votes but slight military power. To prevent a decision that would be against its vital interests, either of these two elements must normally marshal at least seven votes in order to prevent a two-thirds majority on the other side. This Latin America can easily do, thereby effectively preventing the United States from imposing its will on any issue of general and vital concern to the twenty republics. On the other hand, the United States has felt that on any issue affecting its national security it could count on the support of at least seven Latin American countries, either in the form of negative votes or abstentions, to prevent a decision it would find unacceptable. It will be noted that each side has reasonable protection *against* collective decisions unfavorable to it. It follows that there is no guarantee that either side can ever be assured of obtaining the *positive* decisions which it desires.

The political framework for the collective security system in the hemisphere is thus clearly set forth in the Treaty of Rio de Janeiro. The treaty, however, establishes no form of military cooperation or system of military forces under collective command. The reasons for this omission, and the consequences, will be discussed later. The absence of any provision for military forces under collective command is one of the main differences between the inter-American security system and that of the United Nations and of Nato.

## 5. The Charter of Bogotá

Although it followed the Treaty of Rio de Janeiro by one year, the Charter of the O.A.S. is the true constitution of the regional organization. This extraordinary document, the contents of which range all the way from the statement of broad philosophical and humanitarian principles to relatively minor details of procedure, was drafted at an extraordinary conference. The Ninth International Conference of American States was held in the spring of 1948 in Bogotá, Colombia. Its main accomplishments were the drafting of two treaties: the Charter of the O.A.S. and the American Treaty of Pacific Settlement (known as the Pact of Bogotá). In the achievement of these tasks the conference crowned decades of thought and experience on the principles and procedures of inter-American relations. In this respect the conference, and the charter it produced, were retrospective. But in other respects the Bogotá Conference was a foreshadowing of what was to come.

On April 9, shortly after the conference got under way, a popular Colombian political leader, Jorge Eliécer Gaitán, was assassinated. Mobs of his followers, consisting mainly of the humbler elements among the population, rose in a demonic outburst of angry violence. For twenty-four hours they subjected Bogotá and several other cities of the country to a holocaust of fire, looting, killing, and destruction. A large part of the downtown section of the Colombian capital was devastated; the government was almost overthrown; many foreign delegations were isolated overnight amidst raging fires; and control over the city was finally regained by the army which, by mere coincidence it seems, had been stationed outside of the city on some routine maneuvers the very day that hell broke loose.

The riots which shook the city, and in fact the whole Republic of Colombia, were an expression of profound frustration on the part of the Colombian masses. Having seen their demands for the improvement of their miserable conditions disregarded, postponed, or shelved time and again by one so-called "democratic" government after another, they thought that at long last they had found in Gaitán a leader who would be able to make the government respond to their needs and desires. When he was snatched away by the assassin's bullet, the mob jumped to the conclusion (which was never proved) that the Conservative administration then in power was responsible for the murder. Their violence turned first against the government and the ruling Conservative party—and then, it seemed, against anyone and anything that symbolized authority and order. The riots of April 9 were prophetic of what was to come to pass in greater or lesser degree in other parts of Latin America, as the masses became more and more disillusioned with existing governments— whether dictatorships or so-called democracies—and gave vent to their frustrations. One of the participants in the Bogotá riots was a young Cuban law student and revolutionary named Fidel Castro.

Once law and order had been restored, the conference resumed its deliberations, albeit under severe physical limitations because of the destruction of property. And on May 2, 1948, in the Quinta de Bolívar, the Charter of the O.A.S. was signed. The setting permits a bit of fanciful speculation as to whether the spirit of the Liberator may not have smiled to see how much of his original thought had finally been incorporated in a document bringing together the republics of the hemisphere a century and a quarter after his own imaginative but abortive effort.

To North Americans, accustomed to the relatively dry and practical terms in which our own constitutions are written, the Charter of the O.A.S. is an amazing composite of rules, agreements, principles, and aspirations. In keeping with Latin American sentiments, the document not only sets forth what the member countries agree should be the structure and procedures of their organization, but gives the emotional motive power to the machine as well. The Charter is therefore a body of doctrine as well as a constitution. The first eight chapters that compose Part I include virtually every basic inter-American principle that has received popular and official support since the early nineteenth century. Some of these declarations seem to be pure rhetoric to the more literal Anglo-Saxon mind. For example: "The spiritual unity of the continent is based on respect for the cultural values of the American countries and requires their close cooperation for the high purposes of civilization." But even these rhetorical phrases have carried the seeds of important future development. One such article reads: "The solidarity of the American States and the high aims which are sought through it require the political organization of those States on the basis of the effective exercise of representative democracy." We will have occasion to return to this point later.

Of special importance are the principles reflecting the historic struggle over intervention and nonintervention. In Article 15 of the Charter the principle of nonintervention receives its most absolute expression:

> No State or group of States has the right to intervene, directly or indirectly, for any reason whatever, in the internal or external affairs of any other State. The foregoing principle prohibits not only armed force but also any other form of interference or attempted threat against the personality of the State or against its political, economic and cultural elements.

The basic idea is reinforced in other articles and in other words, especially Article 17 regarding the use of military force. However, Article 19 states:

Measures adopted for the maintenance of peace and security in accordance with existing treaties do not constitute a violation of the principles set forth in Articles 15 and 17.

Part II of the Charter deals with the Organization itself, setting forth the hierarchy of "organs" through which the O.A.S. does its work. The member governments have delegated authority to these organs with great reserve, and in doing so have seemed to prefer those of a representative, rather than executive, character. Chief among them is the Inter-American Conference, which is to be held every five years. Then comes the Meeting of Consultation of Ministers of Foreign Affairs, which is to meet when called "to consider problems of an urgent nature and of common interest . . . and to serve as Organ of Consultation."

The Council of the Organization is the only representative organ established by the Charter that meets in permanent session. We may pause for a moment to consider just what its powers are. Like other features of the O.A.S., the Council is the product of a long evolution under the influence of powerful political forces, both positive and negative.

By the time of the adoption of the Charter of the O.A.S. it had become clear that the Organization would require some permanent body, on which all countries would have equal representation, to carry out a number of tasks, in addition to the supervision of the Pan American Union which had previously been performed by the old Governing Board. There was a move on the part of the more enthusiastic internationalists to create a political council broadly empowered to consider any matter related to the effective functioning of the Inter-American System and the solidarity and general welfare of the American republics. On the other side were those who viewed with alarm the granting of political powers to a body located in Washington and therefore subject to the real or imagined control of the United States. Supporters of the more radical plan, therefore, urged another device to ensure the greater independence of the Council: the requirement that the representatives on the Council should not be diplomatic representatives accredited to the government of the United States. It was argued that no diplomat responsible for conducting the relations of a Latin American government with the United States could be expected to oppose the United States in the Council on issues of prime importance to the latter. A provision for such *ad hoc* representation had been adopted at the Mexico City Conference of 1945, but had never been carried out because of the inability or unwillingness of some of the smaller countries to maintain two representatives of ambassadorial rank in Washington.

Not even such a plan—or another related one to provide for a peripatetic Council, meeting each year in a different capital to avoid the influence of any one government—was satisfactory to the conservative group. They argued for an outright prohibition against the exercise of political powers by the Council. At last a compromise was achieved: the Council was not given any outright grant of political powers in the Charter; nor was any prohibition on such powers adopted.

The Council as it now stands derives its powers from three main sources: the Charter, the Treaty of Rio de Janeiro, and the American Treaty of Pacific Settlement. Under the Charter the Council "takes cognizance, within the limits of the present Charter and of inter-American treaties and agreements, of any matter referred to it by the Inter-American Conference or the Meeting of Consultation of Ministers of Foreign Affairs" (Article 50). This vague grant of authority is obviously subject to interpretation; thus far a strict interpretation has prevailed, and the Council has not considered itself authorized to take up political subjects except under specific assignment by virtue of treaty provisions. The other powers delegated to the Council by the Charter are primarily those of a housekeeping nature, concerned with the supervision of the activities, relationships, and financing of various branches and organs of the O.A.S. The Council also determines the agenda for the Inter-American Conferences and Meetings of Foreign Ministers and prepares proposals for their consideration.

The outstanding grant of political power to the Council comes from the Treaty of Rio de Janeiro. Under that treaty the Council can act provisionally as Organ of Consultation, thus availing itself of all the broad powers inherent in the treaty. Under the American Treaty of Pacific Settlement the Council has certain other minor political functions consisting mainly of seeing to the organization of committees of investigation and conciliation and resolving, when necessary, deadlocks between the parties to a dispute in regard to various procedural steps. The Council has three subordinate bodies, also called councils, with responsibilities of a technical nature in the respective fields of economic and social affairs, juridical problems, and cultural relations.

Other "organs" of the O.A.S. listed in the Charter are the Pan American Union, which is the general secretariat and principal administrative body, and the specialized organizations and conferences. The annual budget of the Pan American Union alone now amounts to more than $10 million. Through its various branches and offices are carried out a number of programs in all fields of inter-American cooperation: juridical studies, cultural exchange, scientific development, and above all economic and social analysis and planning. The Pan American Union is also the central point for public information on the O.A.S. and its activities, a function which has been badly neglected.

The specialized organizations and their respective conferences likewise perform an important, and sometimes spectacular, function. Outstanding among them is the Pan American Health Organization, with an annual budget of about $4.7 million, which has done remarkable work in strengthening the national health services of the member countries and coordinating their efforts in continent-wide campaigns to eradicate disease and promote a more healthful environment. This agency also serves as the regional branch, for the Western Hemisphere, of the World Health Organization. The Inter-American Institute of Agricultural Sciences is another specialized agency of the O.A.S. with an impressive record and a far greater potential for developing the knowledge and techniques needed for the modernization and improvement of Latin American agriculture. Other specialized agencies have to do with history and geography, child welfare, the political and social status of women, and indigenous populations.

Despite their enthusiasm for the regional concept, the American republics have actually approached the delegation of power to the regional organization with great reserve. The Charter of the O.A.S. was adopted three years after the United Nations Charter, which had been ratified by all the member states of the O.A.S. Yet there are significant differences with respect to the delegation of power. The O.A.S. has, it will be seen from the foregoing résumé, no general organ, equivalent to the U.N. General Assembly, in which any matter of common interest can be raised. The nearest approach is the Inter-American Conference, which meets as a rule only once in five years and is limited by the time at its disposal as well as by the procedures for the preparation of the agenda. Nor is there any body like the Security Council, where any controversy likely to disturb the peace can be raised. The Meeting of Consultation of Ministers of Foreign Affairs is the nearest parallel, yet this group of high officials obviously cannot be called together whenever a dispute between two member states arises. The Council of the O.A.S. has no power to hear political controversies unless aggression takes place or is threatened, in which case it must call a Meeting of Consultation as provided under the Treaty of Rio de Janeiro. The Secretary-General is not authorized, as is his counterpart in the United Nations, to call the attention of the O.A.S. to situations threatening the peace.

Yet the O.A.S. did not come into being at Bogotá without a plethora of organs, agencies, and instrumentalities. There are councils and subcouncils, committees and subcommittees. There are technical agencies, institutes, and all kinds of administrative units within or related to the Pan American Union. In fact, one major problem is the maze of organs which absorb incredible amounts of time, human energy, and material resources, and yet often complicate and delay the taking of decisions and action.

## 6. *The Inter-American Peace System*

The Treaty of Rio de Janeiro and the Charter are the two main pillars of the O.A.S. structure today. A third basic document, to which both the other two make reference, is the American Treaty of Pacific Settlement, or Pact of Bogotá. Its adoption culminated more than a century of effort by the Latin American states to make effective their desire to ban the use of force in their international controversies and to settle disputes by peaceful means.

The Pact of Bogotá brings together in one document all the recognized procedures of pacific settlement: good offices, mediation, investigation and conciliation, arbitration and judicial settlement. It defines the steps by which each of these procedures can be set in motion, and gives to the Council of the O.A.S. certain responsibilities to see that the machinery, once called into action, proceeds to work. The treaty, however, suffers from the same ailment as some of the earlier efforts to create an inter-American peace system—perfectionism. It obligates the parties to a tight regimen whereby all disputes that may arise between them and cannot be settled by direct negotiation must necessarily be submitted to one after the other of the various procedures set forth in the treaty. The United States and several other countries have objected to some of its provisions and have therefore not ratified the Pact of Bogotá, even though they are sympathetic to its purpose. Nine of the American states have now ratified the treaty, and it is in effect among them.

Of greater importance to the peaceful settlement of inter-American disputes has been the Inter-American Peace Committee, made up of representatives of five governments chosen by the Council. It is an ironic fact that this highly useful organ was completely overlooked in the drafting of the Charter of the O.A.S. as well as in the Pact of Bogotá. Established by resolution of the Second Meeting of Consultation of Ministers of Foreign Affairs in Havana in 1940, the Committee was given the duty of "keeping constant vigilance to insure that States between which any dispute exists or may arise . . . may solve it as quickly as possible . . . and of suggesting the measures and steps that may be conducive to a settlement." It has consistently and scrupulously abided by this limited grant of powers. It has made clear that it has no authority to judge disputes or issue opinions upon the merits of a case presented to it. Nor is it authorized under the Havana resolution to propose formulas of settlement or even to mediate between the parties. Far less does the Peace Committee have any authority to compel any government to act or refrain from acting as it chooses. Its only authority is moral.

Yet the very weakness of the Inter-American Peace Committee has been the cause of its success in bringing together conflicting parties and helping them to resolve acute controversies peacefully. Since the Committee has no power to enforce any decision upon a government, it is hard for any government to feel that its position is endangered by coming before it. Experience has shown that the Peace Committee can fill a useful and necessary role when two governments, which basically have no wish to resort to force, find themselves embroiled in a controversy which could easily be settled if they could only be brought together without either one losing face. This the Peace Committee has done. In the thirteen years of its existence it has helped to resolve a number of controversies, some of which had reached the boiling point and threatened to break out into armed conflict.

As recently as 1961 the Inter-American Peace Committee added a new laurel to its crown in a case which at one time or another had called for the services of all the main organs of the O.A.S. collective security system. In 1957 the Treaty of Rio de Janeiro was brought into play in the conflict between Honduras and Nicaragua over their boundary. The Council, acting provisionally as Organ of Consultation, dispatched a committee to the scene and was able to bring about a cessation of hostilities. The two governments then agreed that in accordance with the Pact of Bogotá they would submit their old controversy to the International Court of Justice. After the Court issued an opinion supporting the claims of Honduras, the problem was how to arrange the transfer of territory from the *de facto* control of Nicaragua, the movement of people, disposition of property, and the final clarification of a few cloudy sections in the delimitation of the boundary. In the face of these thorny problems relations between the two governments again became strained. They then turned to the Inter-American Peace Committee for assistance, asking it to supervise the execution of the Court's decision. The Committee agreed, and in August 1961 final disposition was made of a dispute that had existed since colonial days and had constituted a recurrent irritant in the relations of the two Central American republics.

## 7. Conclusion

This brief summary of the development of the O.A.S. has sought to emphasize a few salient points about this international instrument of the American republics. Of the greatest importance is the fact that it evolved out of the history of the new world, and that historical forces are very much present today in its doctrines, structure, and methods of work. The process which brought forth the O.A.S. as it exists today, on the basis of the treaties of Rio de Janeiro and Bogotá, represents the resolution of two powerful and often conflicting forces. One has been the pressure of the Latin American countries for an ideal form of international association reflecting the Bolivarian concept of a league of equal partners whose major policies and actions in matters of common concern should be determined by consultation and multilateral decision. The other force has been the expanding influence of the United States as it grew in size and strength, and its tendency to seek pragmatic solutions for hemisphere problems through the use of its own power and resources, particularly when it came to protecting the security of the hemisphere.

The fact that the institutions, obligations, and procedures set forth in the two basic treaties underlying the O.A.S. were, in 1947 and 1948, freely established by a group of nations of such disparate size, power, and interests as the United States on the one hand and the Latin American countries on the other is evidence that there existed at that time sufficient mutual confidence in their common purposes to overcome the obstacles imposed by the obvious differences. The successful collaboration during the war years, and the expectation that the constructive relationship thus established would continue to the benefit of all parties, no doubt had much to do with the important political decisions that were implicit in the Latin American position at San Francisco, Rio de Janeiro, and Bogotá. For had the Latin American countries at that time felt a distrust of the motives of the United States, as had been the case during the period of interventions in the early twentieth century, they might well have sought in 1945 to merge their interests in the larger grouping of the United Nations, to seek safety in numbers, and to solicit the protection of other world powers which might not be averse to checking the influence of the United States. Such a policy is, in fact, sometimes advocated by critics of the Inter-American System who favor a Pan Latin American movement instead.[4] The Latin American countries in 1947 and 1948, however, clung to the Pan American approach, apparently convinced that such a course offered a greater opportunity for progress in matters of major concern to them.

The United States on its part, by accepting the far-reaching commitments involved in the new O.A.S., moved again toward a wider sharing of its authority and responsibility with the other states of the hemisphere. Despite the strong pull of the "one world" philosophy that lay at the basis of the United Nations, the United States was not prepared to abandon the regional association that had proved so valuable in wartime. By 1948, portents of the growing controversy with the Soviet Union had revived attention to the importance of continental solidarity. Moreover, increasingly involved in problems in other parts of the world, the United States saw in the O.A.S. an opportunity to create in the Western Hemisphere a relatively calm and orderly international community

---

[4] See, for example, Jorge Castañeda, *Mexico and the United Nations* (New York: Manhattan Publishing Co., for El Colegio de México and the Carnegie Endowment for International Peace, 1958), Chapter 7.

which might act as a stabilizing influence in the larger world picture.

Adoption of treaties can regulate, but hardly eliminate, the underlying political and economic factors that in the last analysis determine the policies of governments. Nor does the establishment of international agencies by any means assure their success. The performance of the O.A.S., like that of any other broad international political arrangement, is governed by the basic dynamics of the relations of its member states. How the Organization, as set up in Rio de Janeiro and Bogotá, climaxing half a century or more of evolutionary development, has worked out in the face of political realities will be considered in the following chapters.

# III

# Protecting
# National Sovereignty

It is no accident that our brief account of the evolution of the
O.A.S. and summary description of its present organization placed
so much emphasis upon its functions and mechanisms associated
with the protection of the sovereignty and independence of the
member states. The guarantee of sovereignty is in fact the major
purpose toward which the energies of the American governments
have until very recently been directed in the development of the
international arrangements embodied in the Treaty of Rio de
Janeiro and the Charter. While other purposes have been stated—
such as the promotion of economic and social progress and the
protection of human liberties—they have played a minor role in
the operations of the O.A.S. until very recently. It is in the protection
of the sovereignty and independence of states that the Organization
has achieved its greatest success and won its major plaudits.

Two outstanding accomplishments, as we have seen, contributed
to that success. The first was the adoption of the nonintervention
principle which erected a legal barrier to protect the Latin American
countries from interference by the United States. The second was the
adoption of the Treaty of Rio de Janeiro and the elaboration of its
machinery to enforce the peace and prevent all kinds of aggression.

In this chapter we shall examine the performance of the O.A.S. with respect to the two aspects of the latter function: the defense of the hemisphere from extracontinental aggression, and the maintenance of peace and security among the American republics themselves.

The defense of the hemisphere is concerned with two main types of aggression: military and political. What capacity does the O.A.S. have in each of these areas, and how has it performed?

### *1. Military Defense of the Hemisphere*

In the military defense of the continent, the O.A.S. has served primarily as a vehicle for the coordination of military policy under the leadership of the United States. Reality makes this role virtually inevitable. Even under the relatively simple concepts of conventional warfare that prevailed during the early years of the Second World War, when the hemisphere was seriously thought to be in danger of an attack by the Germans via Africa and the South Atlantic, the United States was virtually the only American state that could play a significant role in military defense. The participation of any of the other countries in significant military operations was entirely dependent upon the equipping and training of their forces by the United States. Thus it was that a program of military cooperation was developed under which the United States attained the objectives it considered essential for its general strategy—such as the establishment of air bases in northeast Brazil for ferrying planes to the African and European theaters of war—and provided certain training and equipment to the military forces of Latin American countries. Brazil and Mexico, moreover, sent contingents to the combat areas, while they and other Latin American countries assumed limited missions in the defense of the continent and adjacent seas.

With the development of atomic weapons and missile warfare, the preponderance of the United States in military matters became even more overwhelming. Yet under the Treaty of Rio de Janeiro the responsibility for hemisphere defense is clearly shared by all the American republics. Some means must be found to retain in the military defense of the continent the political ingredient of mutuality that is the essence of the O.A.S. One obvious method is regular consultation between the United States and its sovereign partners on defense matters. In the realm of general policy and for the critical situations it is called together to consider, the Meeting of Consultation of Ministers of Foreign Affairs serves this purpose. For continuing consultation on strictly military matters there is the Inter-American Defense Board, with its headquarters in Washington.

The organization and functioning of the Inter-American Defense Board are conditioned upon the military superiority of the United States and, therefore, upon its predominant responsibility for the military defense of the continent. The Board was organized as a wartime measure in 1942 and has not changed its fundamental character since that time. The armed forces of all the member states of the O.A.S. are normally represented on the Board (Cuba, at the time of writing, is excluded), and other officers are detailed by the respective governments to serve on its staff. The regulations of the Board provide that the chairman, the director of the staff, and the secretary shall be members of the armed forces of the host country (i.e., the United States), while for each of these officers there is a deputy who is elected from among the Latin American countries. While the Board conducts its work by studies, debates, and votes, the guiding influence rests in the hands of the United States.

This predominance of the United States in the military agency of the O.A.S. no doubt contributes to more efficient arrangements for continental defense. The political consequences of this situation, however, did not escape the attention of Latin American political leaders who are justifiably sensitive to the powerful political role that the armed forces play in their respective countries. The establishment of an inter-American agency for the ostensible purpose of assuring the more effective defense of the hemisphere could easily bring increased prestige and power to the military elements in each state. And it was seen that if the United States were to exercise its great power and influence in presiding over this agency, the possibility of political intervention by the United States in Latin American affairs through the military channel might become dangerous. The Latin American nations therefore made sure to diminish this potential danger to the nonintervention principle by severely circumscribing the powers and responsibilities of the Inter-American Defense Board.

The Board deals only with problems of hemisphere defense; it has no responsibilities for the defense of any member state against attacks other than those originating from outside the continent. Thus it is carefully excluded from dealing with the touchy problems that would be involved in planning the military defense of one Latin American country against a hypothetical attack from a neighbor. Nor does a related problem of equal delicacy come within the Board's competence: the level of armaments in individual countries. The Board may recommend plans it considers necessary or desirable in the interests of hemisphere defense, but it cannot go so far as to stipulate what kind of or how large a military establishment is needed by any country. For, in addition to whatever task it should perform in the defense of the continent, each country has other—and to it perhaps more immediate—problems of national defense against its neighbors which it must take into account in determining the size and composition of its armed forces.

The Inter-American Defense Board is, moreover, only a technical advisory and consultative body. Its duty is to recommend measures for the common defense to the member governments. These plans or recommendations have no validity unless accepted by the member governments, and each may therefore be said to have a virtual veto on any defense plans applying to it. Of even greater significance to the O.A.S. as a whole is the fact that the Defense Board has no authority—as does, technically, the Military Staff Committee of the United Nations—to organize forces or establish a unified command. There are no military forces available to the Inter-American Defense Board—or to any other branch of the O.A.S.—either in being or on paper; nor is there any constitutional provision for the organization of such forces, whether for hemisphere defense or any other purpose. The nonmilitary character of the O.A.S. is indicated by the fact that the only reference to military affairs appearing in the Charter concerns the creation of an Advisory Defense Committee which is to meet only on special convocation, notably to give advice in connection with the consideration of military measures to be taken under the Treaty of Rio de Janeiro. This committee has in fact never been organized.

What function, then, does the Defense Board in reality perform? Its role is essentially threefold: to promote a sense of solidarity among the top officers of the military forces of the American states; to engender an understanding of the collective problems of the defense of the hemisphere; and to provide a multilateral basis for defense measures that may be adopted unilaterally or bilaterally by member countries, especially, of course, the United States. Any action that results from the deliberations of the Board is left to the governments to carry out, either unilaterally or by special agreement with each other. In practice the United States, as the only member state of the O.A.S. capable of providing significant amounts of military equipment, has signed bilateral military agreements with most of the Latin American countries. Under these accords, certain military equipment is made available for the execution of the confidential military missions which, under the basic concepts approved by the Defense Board, the recipient country is supposed to execute in case of an attack against the hemisphere.

In this connection it is interesting to recall how it happened that no standing military agency was provided for in the Charter of the O.A.S. The draft charter that was prepared by the Governing Board of the Pan American Union in 1948 envisaged a Council with four subordinate technical organs to deal respectively with economic, cultural, juridical, and military matters. The Conference at Bogotá adopted the plan insofar as the three civilian bodies were concerned but omitted the defense council. Opposition to this feature of the plan was led by the Mexican delegation. While political considerations of the kind mentioned earlier no doubt had an important, if unspoken, influence on this position, the formal arguments against the establishment of the projected military council were typically juridical. Since the O.A.S. was not a traditional military alliance, the Mexican authorities argued, it was inappropriate for the Organization to have a permanent military agency; in fact, to create one would invade the sphere of the United Nations, which had the responsibility for enforcing international peace. All that was needed in the O.A.S., they maintained, was an advisory military group which could be called together in case military action should be needed to repel an armed attack against a member state. However, recognizing that existing world conditions made it advisable to have some agency capable of planning continental defense measures in advance, the Mexican delegation agreed to continue the Inter-American Defense Board by means of a resolution until such a time as two-thirds of the member states should decide to abolish it.

The statement of its position by the Mexican delegation provided a dramatic incident at the Bogotá Conference. The issue of whether to include a defense council in the Charter, and what its position in the Organization should be, had been referred to a committee of delegation heads, who in turn called on their military advisers for an opinion. The proposal for the establishment of a defense council was endorsed by the military advisers of the United States and the participating Latin American countries except Mexico. After others had spoken at the small meeting, it was the turn of the Mexican general. Standing behind him in the crowded room was the Mexican Foreign Minister, who headed his country's delegation. Quietly the Mexican general said that, while he personally was in agreement with his military colleagues from the other countries, his government had adopted a contrary position and that, as Mexico's representative, he must oppose the creation of the permanent military body. To anyone familiar with the political power of the military in the governments of the Latin American countries, this incident was a striking illustration of the degree to which the Mexican government had established the supremacy of civilian political authority even in military aspects of foreign policy.

For military defense, then, the treaty obligations were clear, but the inter-American machinery for planning and operations was hardly substantial. From the standpoint of the realities, of course, the military tasks and decisions were bound to fall to the United States. What was important was the atmosphere of mutuality and political cooperation in which those decisions would be taken. It was even more important in the field of political defense against penetration and indirect aggression, for here the role of the Latin American nations was inevitably much greater.

## 2. *Political Defense*

If the member states were reluctant to grant effective powers to the O.A.S. in military defense, they were equally hesitant when it came to the field of political defense. The wartime Third Meeting of Foreign Ministers, held at Rio de Janeiro in 1942, established an Emergency Advisory Committee for Political Defense to "study and coordinate the measures" that the conference recommended for the purpose of controlling the subversive activities of the Axis powers. This committee was unprecedented in two ways. Functionally, it was unique in having the authority to delve into matters that were directly related to the internal political situation in each country: such ticklish questions as the control by governments of individuals, including their own citizens, within their respective territories. By skillful dealing and careful avoidance of any assumption that it could impose its views on governments, the Committee made great strides in encouraging, stimulating, and guiding the adoption of effective measures of control.

The Committee for Political Defense, with its seat at Montevideo, was also unique in an organizational sense. Established by all twenty-one governments (although Argentina under Perón withdrew from participation and cooperation with it), the Committee actually consisted of only seven members designated by governments selected by the then Governing Board of the Pan American Union. These seven members were instructed to consider themselves as acting in the interests of all twenty-one countries in their consideration of hemisphere problems. It was possible by this means to establish an effective group and to avoid the cumbersome machinery of a committee of twenty-one representatives of sovereign powers.

The very uniqueness of the Committee for Political Defense was the cause of its abandonment at the Bogotá Conference. The government of Uruguay, both as host to the Committee and as a traditional champion of democracy and human rights, proposed that the Committee be continued with the duty of recommending measures to the governments for the promotion of human rights and perfection of democratic institutions. The answer of the Latin American governments was a resounding "no." By 1948 the tide of democracy had begun to recede and military dictators had taken over the governments in several countries. They wanted nothing to do with an O.A.S. body that would "intervene" in their affairs under an international mandate. The limited membership of the Committee made it especially unpalatable, even to governments that were in no sense protagonists of dictatorship.

If the member states do not wish to maintain a special committee for political defense, why cannot the Council of the O.A.S. carry out such responsibilities? As the earlier discussion of its powers makes clear, the Council simply does not have the authority to deal with internal political problems such as those that would be involved in political defense against Communist penetration and aggression (except in an extreme case in which the Treaty of Rio de Janeiro is invoked). This limitation is primarily due to the reluctance of the Latin American governments to place political power that could be exercised in an interventionist manner in the hands of a body that might be subject to an undue influence of the United States. Recent experience has indicated that there is far more shadow than substance to the "influence" which the United States exercises over the Council of the O.A.S. This fact, however, is not widely recognized in Latin America, and fears have a way of dying out slowly.

Fear of U.S. political domination, rather than any sympathy with communism, has been a main reason for the reluctance of the O.A.S. on various occasions, whether in the Council or the Meetings of Consultation of Ministers of Foreign Affairs, to take a stronger position against Communist infiltration and subversion. Defense against communism is recognized as desirable; but this does not, in the Latin American view, justify the risk of opening the door to U.S. political domination. It is a case of "Communism, no! Yankee intervention, also no!"

The O.A.S. has, indeed, declared itself clearly against communism on several occasions—a fact that makes its weakness in action the more incomprehensible to North Americans. The Bogotá Conference in 1948 adopted a strong declaration against communism, declaring "that, by its anti-democratic nature and its interventionist tendency, the political activity of international communism or any other totalitarian doctrine is incompatible with the concept of American freedom. . . ." The signatories resolved "to adopt, within their respective territories and in accordance with their respective constitutional provisions," the measures necessary to eradicate and prevent Communist activities directed from abroad. This resolution is full of euphemisms and indirect references. Of particular significance was its condemnation of other forms of totalitarianism, which meant fascist and military dictatorships. But the resolution was clear in condemning communism and it urged the control of subversive activities by each country, acting individually within its own territory.

The so-called Caracas Resolution against communism is more widely known. This is Resolution 93 of the Tenth Inter-American Conference (1954), impressively titled "Declaration of Solidarity for the Preservation of the Political Integrity of the American States against the Intervention of International Communism." The approval of this resolution was a significant act in itself. The insistence of the United States on having a strong anti-Communist declaration adopted encountered the reluctance of the Latin American countries to bow to this pressure, lest it in some degree open the door to U.S. intervention. On paper, the United States won the day at Caracas; but, when all is said and done, it is questionable how much progress was actually achieved toward getting the American states to take action against the danger of Communist political penetration.

The Caracas Resolution "condemns the activities of the international communist movement as constituting intervention in American affairs" and expresses the determination of the American states to take the necessary measures to protect their political independence against this force. It then declares, in its major paragraph, that

. . . the domination or control of the political institutions of any American State by the international communist movement, extending to this Hemisphere the political system of an extracontinental power, would constitute a threat to the sovereignty and political independence of the American States, endangering the peace of America, and would call for a Meeting of Consultation to consider the adoption of appropriate action in accordance with existing treaties.

After recommending various measures in the realm of exchange of information and systems of internal control, the Resolution concludes with these words:

This declaration of foreign policy made by the American republics in relation to dangers originating outside this Hemisphere is designed to protect and not to impair the inalienable right of each American State freely to choose its own form of government and economic system and to live its own social and cultural life.

In appraising the value of this resolution, it is necessary to recognize that it is by its own terms a "declaration of foreign policy" and therefore is not to be placed on the same juridical level as a treaty, such as the Treaty of Rio de Janeiro. The Resolution does not, in fact, bind the American governments to anything except the statement of views contained in it.

The meat of the Caracas Resolution is the paragraph, quoted above, in which the governments declare that the domination or control of the political institutions of an American state by the international Communist movement would "call for" a Meeting of Consultation. Article 6 of the Treaty of Rio de Janeiro, it will be recalled, obligates the parties to consult in the event that "the sovereignty or political independence of any American States should be affected by . . . any . . . fact or situation that might endanger the peace of America." What the Caracas Resolution does is to establish in advance that the domination or control of an American state by the "international communist movement," extending to this hemisphere the political system of an extracontinental power, fulfills the requirements for invoking Article 6 of the Treaty of Rio de Janeiro if the American governments wish to do so. It leaves open, however, the question of how this domination or control is to be determined.

Viewed from a strictly practical and technical standpoint, the Resolution may, in fact, have erected a new obstruction in the consideration of the problem of communism in an American republic by introducing the concept of "domination or control of the political institutions." Here is a new juridical barrier behind which the opponents of action can defend a negative policy. Given the reluctance of the Latin American states to undertake any collective action that might be considered as intervention in the affairs of one of their number, particularly on the urging of the United States, it has therefore seemed of doubtful value to invoke the Caracas Resolution. If the will to act is there, it is simpler to do so on the basis of the Treaty of Rio de Janeiro itself.

Political factors have also operated against the use of the Caracas Resolution. It was adopted on the strong insistence of the United States, despite the reluctance of many of the Latin American governments and the outright opposition of some. Its proposal by the United States and a few of the more conservative Latin American governments in 1954 was occasioned, as everyone knew, by the situation in Guatemala, where the Communists had achieved a high degree of influence over the government of President Jacobo Arbenz. Guatemala, naturally, fought hard against the declaration. But so also did Argentina and Mexico—the most dedicated and vigorous exponents of the principle of nonintervention. While the position of Argentina has changed in many respects since that time, with the ousting of Perón and the subsequent internal struggles, Mexico's position today remains the same as at the Caracas Conference with respect to the anti-Communist resolution. Now, as then, Mexico opposes anything which suggests that the O.A.S., no less than any member state, has the right to intervene in what might be considered the internal affairs of another American state. It would oppose any attempt to invoke the Caracas Resolution, if only to maintain a consistent position.

A careful review of the text of the Caracas Resolution will reveal nothing objectionable in it from the standpoint of inter-American doctrine or policy. It rests upon the oldest traditions of the inter-American community: the independence of states and the right of the nations of the new world to live their own life free from political intervention from any extracontinental power. Yet the Resolution, duly approved by more than a sufficient majority of governments, has turned out to be largely ineffectual because, in the last analysis, the Latin American countries have generally been more concerned with its potential danger as a basis for intervention led by the United States than with the danger of Communist intervention in their own affairs. The fact that the conference met under the hospitality of a military dictator, General Pérez Jiménez of Venezuela, who gladly supported the Resolution, and that the United States was at that time widely believed to find military dictators acceptable so long as they were sufficiently anti-Communist, did not help commend the Resolution to the majority of Latin American peoples.

These factors go far to explain why, when the time came to organize action through the O.A.S. in regard to the situation in Guatemala, the United States and the other countries most concerned did not invoke the Caracas Resolution. They resorted directly to the Rio Treaty, avoiding the necessity of having to prove "domination or control" of the political institutions of Guatemala by "the international communist movement." Likewise, in the case of Cuba, in January 1962, the Rio Treaty rather than the Caracas declaration was invoked as the basis of action.

What made it possible to get the problem of Guatemala considered by the O.A.S. was not the doctrine set forth in the Caracas Resolution or any other anti-Communist manifesto, but the sudden arrival in a Guatemalan port of a shipload of arms from behind the iron curtain. This fact shocked much of Latin America into a realization of the close connections between the Arbenz government and the Soviet bloc—a connection which had theretofore been widely disbelieved or dismissed as unimportant. Guatemala's small neighbors, already aroused over Guatemalan political interference in their internal affairs, now became seriously alarmed at the added military threat.

The arms shipment was believed to have substantially altered the balance of military power in Central America. Thus it became possible for other Central American states to join in requesting a Meeting of Consultation of Ministers of Foreign Affairs under Article 6 of the Treaty of Rio de Janeiro. The request was considered in the Council of the O.A.S., where it encountered, of course, the vigorous opposition of Guatemala, which denounced the move as a maneuver by Yankee imperialists to crush the social revolution and restore the fortunes and privileged position of the United Fruit Company. But careful diplomatic preparation by the United States and other interested governments had paved the way for overwhelming approval of a resolution convoking the Meeting of Foreign Ministers, which was to be held in Rio de Janeiro on July 7, 1954.

In the meantime, however, the "invasion" of Guatemala by Colonel Carlos Castillo Armas and his small band had taken place and, after an initial period of desultory action, had picked up speed. After an encounter in which the Guatemalan army demonstrated its unwillingness to fight, Arbenz was forced to resign. Communist influence over the Guatemalan government was thus ended by Guatemalans without assistance from the O.A.S. (although the assistance of other governments, including the United States, was publicly recognized). Plans for the Meeting of Consultation of Ministers of Foreign Affairs were duly set aside, thus depriving the O.A.S. of this first test as an instrument for the protection of the hemisphere from Communist political aggression.

The incident demonstrated that the Treaty of Rio de Janeiro

provides the necessary legal implements with which to consider a case of this sort and, presumably, to take action. More recently, with respect to the problem of the Communist penetration of Cuba, however, it has been made equally clear that the existence of this potentially effective international machinery carries with it no guarantee that it will be used, and that the decision to throw the machinery into action depends far more upon political than legal considerations. Fidel Castro's public confession of Marxist-Leninist faith, and the political perils faced by other Latin American governments as a result of Castro-Communist intervention were the determining factors that led to the decisions against Cuba at Punta del Este in 1962.

The case of Guatemala occupies a special place in the development of the inter-American security system for its bearing upon the relationship of the O.A.S. to the United Nations in the security field. Having ratified the O.A.S. Charter, Guatemala was a member of that Organization. However, she was not technically a party to the Treaty of Rio de Janeiro, since her ratification had never been deposited for reasons relating to her long-standing dispute over British Honduras. Possibly because legal objections might have been raised to its invocation of the Treaty of Rio de Janeiro, and certainly because it felt greater assurances of support in a world body where the Soviet bloc was represented, the Arbenz government did not appeal to the O.A.S. (except for a vacillating and ineffectual approach to the Inter-American Peace Committee) when Colonel Castillo Armas crossed the border from Honduras. Instead it took the matter to the United Nations Security Council. The question then was whether Guatemala was acting in accordance with her rights or whether she was first obliged to seek solution of her problems in the regional organization. Did the O.A.S. have a prior claim on the conflict?

The United Nations Charter recognizes the desirability of regional organizations or arrangements to consider such matters as are appropriate for regional action. States belonging to such regional arrangements are encouraged to seek solution of their international disputes through those channels, or through peaceful methods of their own choosing, before bringing a case to the U.N. Security Council. However, it is clear in various paragraphs of the United Nations Charter that every member state has the right to appeal to the Security Council, and that the Security Council has priority over all other international bodies when it comes to the maintenance of peace and security.

On the other hand, Article 20 of the O.A.S. Charter provides that "all international disputes that may arise between American States shall be submitted to the peaceful procedures set forth in this Charter, before being referred to the Security Council of the United Nations." And the Charter of the O.A.S., in its chapter on collective security, brings in by reference (although indirectly, not by name) the Treaty of Rio de Janeiro. The latter, in Article 2, obligates the parties "to submit every controversy which may arise between them to methods of peaceful settlement and to endeavor to settle any such controversy among themselves by means of procedures in force in the Inter-American System before referring it to the General Assembly or the Security Council of the United Nations." Thus it would seem that any member of the O.A.S. is obliged to bring its controversies with other American republics before the regional organization before going to the United Nations.

The United States and the two Latin American members of the Security Council, Brazil and Colombia, held to the foregoing view when the Guatemalans brought their complaint before that body. They urged that the controversy be referred to the O.A.S. The Soviet Union and Poland held that Guatemala was fully within its rights in coming to the United Nations, and supported Guatemala's request for a U.N. investigation of the charges that the United States, Honduras, and Nicaragua had intervened in her internal affairs. Other non-American members of the Security Council, for political reasons, sided with the United States, but there was no secret to the reluctance of some to turn a deaf ear to Guatemala's appeal.

The outcome of the consideration of the case in the Security Council was not a clear-cut statement on the fundamental legal issue. However, when the Council refused to take substantive action on Guatemala's appeals and awaited a report from the O.A.S., it implicitly adopted the view that a member of the O.A.S. should, in fulfillment of its regional obligations and in the spirit of the U.N. Charter, seek to have the case resolved in the regional organization before bringing it to the Security Council. This precedent was of great political importance, endorsing as it did the agreements reached among the American states in the Rio Treaty and the Charter of the O.A.S.

In 1960, when the Castro government of Cuba asked the U.N. Security Council to investigate its charges that the United States was planning an aggression against Cuba, the precedent of the Guatemalan case played an important role. By that time, the view had become even more firmly established among the Latin American states that a member of the O.A.S. should first bring its controversies to that body. The Seventh Meeting of Consultation of Ministers of Foreign Affairs, convening at San José in August 1960, declared that "all member states of the regional organization are under obligation to submit to the discipline of the inter-American system." Although Cuba's charges against the United States were so vague and so broad that it is doubtful that they made much impression upon the members of the Security Council, that body did, in fact, refrain from taking action on the basis that the O.A.S. was considering the case. It would thus appear that the Security Council has now built up a strong body of precedent for the position that, while all members of the United Nations have the right to be heard by the world organization, those states that are also members of the O.A.S. should first make a reasonable attempt to have disputes between them settled at the regional level, and that the Security Council should refrain from considering an inter-American dispute until the regional organization has had a chance to consider and report on it.

### *3. Maintenance of Continental Peace and Security*

In the last analysis, the question of how much responsibility should be placed upon the regional organization in questions of maintaining international peace and security depends upon the capability of the regional agency to perform that function adequately and in a manner consistent with the principles of the United Nations as well as in conformity with its own standards. In this respect, the Organization of American States deserves a fairly high rating. By and large, its greatest achievement during the postwar period has been in the realm of maintaining peace and security among its members. Moreover, it has done so in its own way, applying methods, procedures, and concepts often quite different from, though not inconsistent with, those of the world organization. In this sense, the O.A.S. has fully justified the idea of establishing a regional organization for the purpose of settling regional problems in a manner satisfactory to its members.

The success of the O.A.S. in maintaining the peace and security of member states has not been limited to preventing wars and stopping incipient armed conflicts. It has also constituted a solid and fundamental contribution to other aims of the inter-American community. International peace is necessary for political stability and the development of liberal, democratic institutions. Nothing gives greater support to a dictator than the opportunity to charge that neighboring states are threatening his country with attack. It has often been pointed out that dictatorships tend to create international tensions and threats to the peace. It is not so readily recognized that the maintenance of a system of collective security is an important step in the creation of a political climate in which democracy can grow. This is not, one may hasten to add, the same as saying that peace assures democracy: nothing assures democracy except the will of a people to live it, but some conditions are more propitious than others, and one of those conditions is international peace.

Effective assurance of collective security likewise has an important bearing upon economic and social progress. One major approach to

Latin American economic development is through economic integration, of which Central America provides an outstanding example. So long as fears of armed attack or other forms of aggression continue among neighboring states, it is obvious that the closer association required for successful economic integration is impossible. And conversely, the collective guarantee of security provides a stronger political basis on which to build the economic relationships which are required for progress toward modern conditions of life.

Finally, Latin America is also beginning to realize how a reliable system of international security can bring some surcease from the heavy costs of maintaining military establishments. The elimination of the economic waste inherent in the maintenance of large armed forces in Latin America will be achieved far more slowly than one would wish. But, as the O.A.S. continues to demonstrate its ability to enforce international peace and security among its member states, the stupidity of continuing to maintain costly military establishments will become increasingly clear, and the possibility of devoting a greater share of the public wealth to economic rather than military purposes will grow.

The successful measures taken by the O.A.S. to put an end to hostilities and restore peace and security have had still another significant result. They have brought the name and the significance of the Organization home to hundreds of thousands of people throughout the continent who had hardly heard of it before. Elaborate conferences marked by brilliant oratory and resounding resolutions have only a momentary impact on public opinion—and then only upon that relatively small part of the public that concerns itself with international affairs. The sending of an O.A.S. "investigating committee" to a trouble spot, with all the publicity that such an event entails, the gathering of military representatives of several countries to work under O.A.S. auspices in the interests of peace, the appearance of officials identified by O.A.S. arm bands, not only in the capitals but also in remote sections of a country, create a far greater impact upon the general public. Headlines in the home papers concerning Argentine or Mexican participation in a peace mission in some distant country where fighting is being stopped and peace restored, make the Organization real to many people to whom talk of international treaties and juridical agreements means nothing. The various actions of the O.A.S. in policing the hemisphere probably did more than any other thing to make its name familiar and favorably known to the people of the twenty-one republics during the 1950s.

It is ironical that the Treaty of Rio de Janeiro, which was looked upon by some, especially in the United States, as essentially designed for defense of the hemisphere from outside attack, has in its application become primarily associated with the maintenance of peace among the American nations themselves. Drafted and signed in 1947, the treaty had hardly come into effect with the deposit of the fourteenth ratification in December 1948, when it was put to its first test. In the last days of that year, Costa Rica called upon the O.A.S. for help in repelling an armed attack on her northwest frontier that had apparently originated in neighboring Nicaragua. The O.A.S. rose to the challenge with commendable speed and decision. It dispatched the first of the "investigating committees" which were to play so important a role in subsequent use of its peace-keeping machinery. Prompt action, solidly supported by the other member states, brought about a cessation of hostilities and the subsequent signing of special agreements between the two governments covering the problems underlying the conflict. As we shall see, the failure of the two countries to make these agreements effective produced a more serious repetition of the aggression five years later. Nevertheless, the O.A.S. came through its first test with flying colors.

Since that time, the Treaty of Rio has been brought into play in regard to six other disputes between American states:

In 1949-50 the O.A.S. considered charges of aggression brought by Haiti against the Dominican Republic, together with countercharges by the latter against Haiti, Cuba, and Guatemala.

In 1955, the O.A.S. dealt with another invasion of Costa Rica from Nicaragua.

In 1957, fighting between Honduras and Nicaragua over their long-standing boundary dispute was terminated by O.A.S. action and a final settlement arranged.

In 1959, two cases were taken up: the invasion of Panama by a band of Cubans; and the attack on Nicaragua by a group of exiles coming from Costa Rica.

In 1960, the O.A.S. applied sanctions for the first time in the case involving aggression by the Dominican Republic against Venezuela.

In 1962, the O.A.S. decided to exclude the Cuban regime of Fidel Castro from participation in the Inter-American System and to apply limited sanctions against Cuba.

In addition, the Rio Treaty has been invoked unsuccessfully four times by countries seeking O.A.S. action, the Council deciding in each case that the situation did not warrant application of the treaty machinery. The remaining case was that of Guatemala in 1954, already described, in which plans for O.A.S. action were abandoned when changed circumstances made it unnecessary.

An important product of these cases, all of them in the Caribbean and Central American area, was the series of decisions affecting the powers of the Council of the O.A.S. As has already been indicated, the Council as such has no power to take up disputes between states. However, when the Treaty of Rio is invoked, and a Meeting of Ministers of Foreign Affairs is convoked as Organ of Consultation, the Council itself can act provisionally as Organ of Consultation. In the first case considered under the treaty it was decided that for the Council so to act a Meeting of Foreign Ministers must first be convoked. Yet in practice it has become clear that if the Council acted quickly and firmly there would often be no need or justification for calling the foreign ministers into session. This dilemma has been resolved by a juridical stratagem characteristic of many of the solutions worked out in the O.A.S. Even though the nature and proportions of the international conflict do not warrant an actual Meeting of the Ministers of Foreign Affairs, the Council, under the formula adopted, convokes a meeting but leaves the date and place to be determined "later." Having legally called the Organ of Consultation into being, the Council converts itself into the provisional organ, takes all necessary steps to cope with the conflict, and then cancels the convocation for the Meeting of Foreign Ministers. With this last act, the Council reverts to its normal state of relative impotence as a political body.

Of the various cases in which the O.A.S. collective security system has functioned, we shall take the conflict between Costa Rica and Nicaragua in 1955 as an illustration. It happens to be one about which the writer can speak from personal experience. It is also one that marked an important political step in the progress of the O.A.S. Just one year earlier the case of Guatemala had somewhat stained the shining armor of the O.A.S. For reasons which were neither always rational nor entirely based on facts, both the Organization and the United States were widely criticized in Latin America and elsewhere because Guatemala had failed to receive protection from the O.A.S. against the unquestioned "invasion" by Castillo Armas; the whole affair was looked upon as a triumph of reaction over the lofty principles inscribed in O.A.S. documents, and as a clear case of U.S. domination.

The case of Costa Rica in the following year had an opposite effect upon public opinion. Here was a democratic government of unquestioned liberal tendencies fighting for its life against reactionary forces backed by a well-known dictator. The speed with which the O.A.S., with the vigorous support of the United States, came to the rescue of Costa Rica's integrity and right of self-determination won wide acclaim at a time when it was much needed. It brought the prestige of the O.A.S. to a high point not only in the hemisphere but in the world at large.

The conflict between Costa Rica and Nicaragua was a micro-war, small in proportions but with most of the features of a typical contemporary politico-military struggle. It had its origins in conflicting political ideologies: the outspoken democracy of Costa Rica and the authoritarianism which existed in Nicaragua at that time. It involved political as well as military moves, since the objective was to overthrow a government and establish in its place one with a greater political affinity for its neighbor. There were both land and air operations, and bombing attacks that had no further purpose than to terrorize the civilian population.

The government of Costa Rica had received indications for some time in advance that a plan to invade its territory from Nicaragua might be under way and so advised the Council of the O.A.S.[1] The attack came on January 11, 1955. On the same day a meeting of the Council was held and the Treaty of Rio de Janeiro invoked. Under the previously established formula, a Meeting of Consultation of Ministers of Foreign Affairs was called, without fixing the date and place, and the Council proceeded to act "provisionally" with the full powers of the treaty. A committee was established "to conduct an on-the-spot investigation of the pertinent facts and submit a report thereon." This committee, composed of representatives of five countries,[2] was organized immediately. At 6:00 A.M. on the following day its members were airborne on a U.S. military plane bound for Costa Rica, where they arrived the next morning to be greeted as saviors by a cheering crowd of officials and general public.

The first function of the committee was to find out what was actually going on, a task that required the patient winnowing of grains of truth from a mass of misleading chaff. To this end, the Council called upon the member governments of the O.A.S. "that were in a position to do so" to make available to the committee aircraft to conduct "peaceful observation" flights over the area involved in the conflict. Responding promptly to this request, the United States, through the Caribbean Defense Command at the Panama Canal, made available naval patrol craft and some jet fighters. The committee sought to establish two things: the location and nature of the invading forces, and the origin of the invading troops, aircraft, and their supplies. First an observation flight was made by jet fighters

[1] Full documentary reports on this and other cases involving the use of the Treaty of Rio de Janeiro are found in *Applications of the Inter-American Treaty of Reciprocal Assistance, 1948-1956* (Washington: Pan American Union, 1957).

[2] Brazil, Ecuador, Mexico, Paraguay, and the United States.

over all airfields in Nicaragua, the committee believing that this show of "peaceful" air activity under O.A.S. management would impress those responsible for any possible assistance to the invading force. Then a constant observation patrol was organized over those parts of the border where the major hostilities were taking place. Aided by these operations, the committee quickly established beyond reasonable doubt that the "aggressor" forces had come across the border from Nicaragua, and that this was, therefore, an international conflict rather than merely an internal political outbreak in Costa Rica as the Nicaraguan sources had claimed.

The reaction of the other member governments of the O.A.S. to this prompt action, and to the request for assistance, was almost unanimously positive and prompt. Ecuador, Mexico, and Uruguay, in addition to the United States, made aircraft available to the committee. The reluctance of Argentina (then under Perón) and Venezuela (then under Pérez Jiménez) to aid the cause of Costa Rican democracy was brushed aside.

A decisive meeting of the Council was called by the Chairman at 2:00 A.M. on Sunday, January 16, 1955, to consider the Costa Rican government's appeal for military assistance. There was great reluctance on the part of many governments to call forth military forces and thereby widen the hostilities. The United States was asked what it could do. The reply was that the United States would do nothing to supply military assistance unless the O.A.S. so requested; if requested, the United States was prepared to make four fighter aircraft available to Costa Rica at once, negotiations for the sale of these planes having been initiated before the outbreak of hostilities. The Council, in a masterpiece of veiled language and only after long and bitter debate, then adopted a resolution asking "the Governments of the Member States of the Organization to expedite the orders for the purchase of aircraft that Costa Rica may have placed with them." The four combat planes from the United States arrived in San José the next day and soon radically changed the military picture.

The handling of this small incident was significant in that it served to accomplish the necessary end of enabling the United States to provide immediate and adequate military assistance, while subordinating the U.S. action to the legally voiced request of the O.A.S. The limited nature of the military assistance also avoided the danger of broadening the conflict by the entry into combat of additional land forces. The successful O.A.S. action was possible, of course, only because it had the support both of the United States and of the great majority of Latin American countries.

The relations of the O.A.S. and its committee with the government of Nicaragua are of special interest, as they reflect the benefits of the O.A.S. way of dealing with some of the particularly delicate aspects of an intrafamily conflict. The Nicaraguan government officially asserted its innocence and adopted a policy of maintaining formally correct relations with the O.A.S. throughout. When the committee of investigation visited Managua, President Anastasio Somoza received them cordially and arranged to permit the O.A.S. military observers to establish themselves in the border area of Nicaragua. Between the Nicaraguan government and the committee an unacknowledged duel then took place—unacknowledged because the amenities were strictly observed on both sides. Although the committee became fully convinced, and later had full evidence to support the conviction, that the Nicaraguan authorities were deeply involved in the whole operation in violation of treaty commitments, no attempt to convict the Nicaraguan government was made in any O.A.S. body. On the contrary, every effort was made to leave the door open for Nicaragua to cooperate with the O.A.S.—an effort reinforced on the one hand by the ebbing fortunes of the invading forces, and on the other by the solid front of Latin American and U.S. support for the steps taken through the O.A.S.

There were many maneuvers in this duel, including attempts to scare the committee into retreating from its firm position that the fighting must cease and forces be withdrawn, as well as efforts to promote a political deal that would have salvaged some of the purposes of the invasion. But the members of the O.A.S. were able to remain firm, primarily because of the trump card they held in the sanctions that could be voted by the Council under the Rio Treaty at any moment should events not proceed in the right way. At one point, its patience exhausted, the committee announced its intention of returning to Washington to demand the public conviction of Nicaragua as an aggressor and the imposition of sanctions. It abandoned this threat a few hours before its scheduled departure when news came that the invading forces were departing from Costa Rican territory and returning to Nicaragua where they were being "interned."

The policy of permitting Nicaragua to come back into the family with its dignity intact was not adopted without considerable debate. Some governments felt that public condemnation and punishment could not be avoided in the face of facts that had come to the committee's knowledge. However, calmer counsels prevailed. It was the strong desire of the O.A.S. to restore peaceful and, so far as possible, normal relations between the two countries. Condemnation and punishment would have made that impossible. And only the restoration of direct negotiations could, in the last analysis, solve the underlying problems that had created the conflict.

Once the crisis was over, negotiations between Costa Rica and Nicaragua were resumed under the stimulus and the watchful eye of the O.A.S. Council. After several months the two governments signed a new pact of friendship, putting into effect certain provisions that had been advocated five years earlier when the first conflict had taken place. This time, the efforts of the O.A.S. met with a more lasting success.

It will be noted that, in relating the performance of the O.A.S. in this case, no reference is made to any permanent military organization. Since the Inter-American Defense Board is by design exclusively concerned with hemisphere defense, it could not be called upon to play any part in the Costa Rican case. The O.A.S. committee did, however, need a limited number of military officers and men for important duties, especially those of conducting observation flights, manning observation posts along the inadequately marked border, and arranging for the orderly reoccupation of Costa Rican territory by that country's hastily organized army. To accomplish these tasks, the committee set up a group of military advisers, each member of the committee designating one military officer. The ranking member of the military group was a U.S. army colonel who was automatically chosen by his colleagues to preside over the group on the basis of rank, thus facilitating necessary liaison with the United States Caribbean Defense Command in the Panama Canal Zone. A number of military men from all five countries on the committee participated in the work of observation and reporting. As the need for their services decreased, the men were released, and within a month after the committee left Costa Rica to return to Washington the whole military set-up was liquidated. It is doubtful whether the military necessities, limited as they were, could have been more efficiently or economically attended to. Back of it all was, of course, the essential logistical support of the Caribbean Defense Command, which worked with a most commendable efficiency and self-effacement.

The pattern of O.A.S. action that was initiated in 1949 and developed in the case of Costa Rica in 1955 worked effectively again in 1957 in the border conflict between Honduras and Nicaragua. The smooth sailing that characterized the O.A.S. action in these cases was due in part to past experience and to the clarification of procedures for applying the Treaty of Rio de Janeiro. Even more important was the fact that prompt action by the Organization to stop hostilities and restore normal relations between states was, in these cases, fully in accord with the most powerful forces affecting Latin American public and official opinion. In each case action by the O.A.S. to prevent or stop hostilities furthered the cause of political democracy and economic progress. In all cases the ultimate goal of pacific settlement of inter-American disputes was realized. The collective machinery of the O.A.S. contributed in most cases to a strengthening of the cherished nonintervention principle. The active and often leading role of the United States was not resented. Backed by these deeply rooted forces, the O.A.S. machinery worked smoothly and effectively, giving the world a happy demonstration of how a regional collective security system could work.

## 4. The Machinery Stalls

Trouble began to appear on the horizon in 1959, however, when the peace of the Caribbean was again broken by a wave of uprisings, most of them direct sequels to the Castro revolution in Cuba and allegedly aimed at overthrowing dictatorial governments. The case of Panama, where a band of misguided Cuban revolutionaries landed on the shores of the Isthmus in an abortive invasion attempt, serving the interest of disgruntled Panamanian politicians, was effectively dealt with along established lines. The O.A.S. task was made easy by the fact that the Panamanian government could in no sense be considered a dictatorship, and by Fidel Castro's decision to disclaim the venture and call upon the invading *barbudos* to give themselves up.

It was a different story when the Nicaraguan government, in May of 1959, called for help from the O.A.S. after an airborne invasion by a group of conservative exiles who had managed to outwit the authorities in Costa Rica and organize a force in a remote jungle area in that country. Nicaragua made no direct charges against any other government, but insinuated that the Castro regime was behind the revolutionary movement. Other members of the O.A.S. were slow to respond to this appeal. Although General Anastasio Somoza, the former dictator of Nicaragua, had been dead for three years, and his son, Luis Somoza, who had succeeded to the presidency, was making what many people considered a genuine and laudable attempt to lead his country toward more democratic ways, there persisted a widespread feeling that, so long as any members of the Somoza family remained in positions of power (the President's brother, Anastasio, Jr., was head of the armed forces), the curse of the dictatorship still hung over the land.

Most of the Latin American countries, now enjoying a greater degree of political democracy than ever before, had no desire to use the power of the O.A.S. to prevent a revolution that appeared to have democratic objectives. The Treaty of Rio de Janeiro, it was held, had been designed to protect the sovereignty and political independence of states from aggression by other states; no one had thought that it would be used to protect an authoritarian government from a popular uprising just because such an uprising, by force of circumstance, had to start in a neighboring country. On this reasoning, action by the O.A.S. against a democratic revolutionary movement, on the pretext that it was dealing with an international conflict, would in fact constitute intervention in purely internal affairs, and in a direction totally opposite to the democratic aspirations of the Latin American peoples. It was a rather involuted interpretation of the inter-American treaties, perhaps, but also a good example of the fact that they are rarely interpreted outside the political environment of the day. Yet members of the O.A.S., despite their distaste for the Nicaraguan regime, were also reluctant to reject the plea of a sister republic and a party to the Treaty of Rio de Janeiro solely on the unproved assumption that the incident in question was more internal than international in character.

In the end the Council invoked the Rio Treaty on the *prima facie* evidence submitted by the Nicaraguan government, and then proceeded to drag its feet in taking action, pending further clarification of just what was going on. A committee was appointed "to gather necessary additional information on the situation . . . so that the Council will be in a position to decide upon the measures it may be advisable to take." This committee, after a leisurely period of work in Washington, proceeded to Central America, visiting Honduras, Nicaragua, and Costa Rica. A large amount of data was assembled about past, current, and potential revolutionary expeditions of Nicaraguan exiles. The committee found evidence that high Cuban officials had supported certain extremist and Communist-infiltrated Nicaraguan revolutionary groups, but nothing sufficient to prove the involvement of any foreign governments as such in actual invasion projects. On hearing the committee's report, the Council, in a lackluster session fully reflecting the members' distaste for the whole affair, adopted a tepid resolution canceling the invocation of the Rio Treaty and piously recommending that the member governments "strengthen the measures designed to maintain peace, observing the principle of non-intervention."

In the same year, a complete breakdown of the O.A.S. security system was only narrowly averted when the Dominican Republic charged Cuba and Venezuela with having organized and supported armed invasions of Dominican territory by sea and air for the purpose of overthrowing the Trujillo government. These invasions had been ruthlessly wiped out by the efficient Dominican forces, which had in the process gathered considerable evidence as to the origin and composition of the expeditions. The Cuban representative in the Council flatly denied the charges, however, as did the Venezuelan, and it became clear that the Dominican demand for a Meeting of Foreign Ministers under the Rio Treaty to punish Cuba and Venezuela would meet with little support.[3] In these circumstances a group of governments, including the United States, proposed a Meeting of Foreign Ministers under Article 39 of the Charter of the O.A.S., rather than the Rio Treaty, to consider the whole problem of Caribbean turmoil. This way out of a highly unpleasant dilemma was quickly seized, since it would offer an opportunity for the member governments to consult without limiting their meeting to the specific Dominican charges or implying that sanctions might be imposed on Cuba. The Fifth Meeting of Consultation of Ministers of Foreign Affairs was accordingly held in Santiago, Chile, in August of 1959.

The use of coercion in the settlement of problems between American states is traditionally repugnant to Latin Americans, the more so when a popular movement or personality is involved as the presumed object. It was hardly surprising, therefore, that when faced at Santiago with the delicate and difficult problems created by the impact of the Castro revolution on the Caribbean area, the O.A.S. sought to meet them by resorting to traditional procedures of peace-

[3] The Cuban representative was Raúl Roa, who shortly thereafter became Castro's foreign minister. It subsequently became generally known that Castro had backed the Dominican invasions, and publicity concerning them even appeared in Cuban periodicals. There was never any confirmation of the charge against the Venezuelan government.

ful persuasion. At the Santiago meeting, the foreign ministers believed that some continuing presence on the part of the O.A.S. in the Caribbean area would have a calming effect on that turbulent scene. For this purpose they turned to the Inter-American Peace Committee instead of utilizing the enforcement machinery of the Rio Treaty.

The Peace Committee was requested to make a broad study of the problems of the Caribbean that had made necessary the Meeting of Consultation and to report to the Eleventh Inter-American Conference (scheduled for 1960 but later indefinitely postponed). It was to give special attention to the question of nonintervention on the one hand, and, on the other, to the importance of encouraging progress toward democratic government. The Committee's study was also to concern itself specifically with the relationship between the denial of human rights and the creation of international tensions. In carrying out these tasks the Committee was once more granted the power of initiative, which had been taken from it three years earlier by the governments that had instructed it, in its new statute, to refrain from exercising even its limited functions without the prior approval of all parties to a dispute or controversy.

For one year the Inter-American Peace Committee devoted itself to its assignment. To gather material for its report, it sent subcommittees to visit the Antilles and the Central American area. Under its instructions, however, before visiting a given country, the Committee was required to obtain the permission of that country's government. No trouble was encountered in obtaining this permission except in the case of Cuba; the Castro government refused to pay any attention to the Committee's communications or to consider the possibility of permitting it to visit the island republic. The Committee did make a brief visit to the Dominican Republic, where it was presented with evidence showing the complicity of the Castro government in the two expeditions launched from Cuba to invade the Dominican Republic in 1959.

The assignments given to the Inter-American Peace Committee by the Santiago Meeting of Foreign Ministers placed it squarely in

the limelight of public attention, and also created a widespread mis-
understanding of its character and of its function in the Caribbean
turmoil. It was widely and erroneously believed that the Peace Committee could judge and condemn governments that were found to be
violating inter-American treaties or resolutions. In fact, the original,
elementary role of the Committee had not been materially altered
except to assign it the duty of preparing a report.[4]

It soon became clear that the optimistic premise on which the
Santiago Meeting of Foreign Ministers had entrusted the Peace Committee with its new duties—namely, that the authority of the O.A.S.,
expressed in the resolutions of the Santiago meeting and supported
by the "presence" of the Committee, would be sufficient to calm
down the Caribbean—was unwarranted. Castro cared nothing for
the O.A.S., which he called a farce. Trujillo likewise paid no heed
to the resolutions on democracy and human rights; when a civilian
plot against his dictatorship was uncovered in January of 1960, an
intensified reign of terror was visited upon that unhappy land.

There was little that the Inter-American Peace Committee could
do in this situation except, in due course, to issue its reports, two of
which proved to be of some importance. One analyzed in general
terms the chronic situation created in the Caribbean region by the
existence of dictatorships and the consequent plotting of exiles in
foreign lands. It stated the thesis that the denial of human rights and
democracy in any American country could not fail to stimulate international tensions, and that inter-American solidarity did and
must, as stated in the Charter of the O.A.S., "require the organization of the states on the basis of the effective exercise of representative
democracy."[5] Then, in a special report dealing with the Dominican
Republic,[6] the Committee stated the conclusion that international

[4] See pp. 37-39, above.

[5] Inter-American Peace Committee, *Special Report on the Relationship between
Violations of Human Rights or the Non-Exercise of Representative Democracy and the
Political Tensions That Affect the Peace of the Hemisphere* (Washington: Pan American
Union, April 14, 1960; mimeographed).

[6] Inter-American Peace Committee, *Report of the Inter-American Peace Committee
on the Case Presented by Venezuela* (Washington: Pan American Union, June 7, 1960;
mimeographed).

tensions in the Caribbean had indeed been aggravated by flagrant and widespread violations of human rights in that country.

The Peace Committee's reports on the Dominican dictatorship were widely applauded both in the United States and in Latin America. But the Committee found it impossible to make any study of or report on the growing Communist menace in Cuba and the alleged interventions of Fidelistas in other Latin American countries. This situation seemed to many people, especially in the United States, to hold far more serious dangers to the basic relationships of the O.A.S. than the repressive acts of the Trujillo regime, however repugnant the latter may have been. Large quantities of data on the Cuban situation were placed before the Peace Committee by the United States, but no action of any kind was taken.

Why was the Inter-American Peace Committee unable to deal with the problem of Cuba? The answer lies in the new and deeper challenge that now faced the O.A.S. as a result of the Cuban revolution and its political repercussions throughout the hemisphere. For the past twenty years the Inter-American System had functioned well in maintaining peace and security among the American republics. Its major task had been to protect the sovereignty of a group of small nations, all of whom were fundamentally dedicated to the maintenance of peace. The greatest concern of Latin Americans was still that the United States might revert to its interventionist policies of an earlier period, and to this end they had fashioned the principle of nonintervention in an ever more absolute and rigid form. But this period had now come to an end, and the O.A.S. machine ground to a stop as it faced the fresh problems of a new revolutionary period. In the following chapters we shall examine the impact of the new revolutionary forces on the O.A.S. and consider its meaning for the future.

# IV

# New Tools for New Tasks

### *1. A Record of Inadequacy*

The successes achieved by the O.A.S. in the prevention of agression and the settlement of international disputes prior to the emergence of the Castro challenge were widely acclaimed. Yet praise of the Organization, in Latin America at least, was offset by the concomitant and repeated criticism of its failure to achieve similar success in the field of economic and social development. Meetings of the various organs of the O.A.S. and other official gatherings of representatives from the member states resounded with vivid descriptions of the economic and social woes of the peoples of Latin America and eloquent pleas that the O.A.S. take action constructively and without delay. While such speeches were sometimes given more with an eye to political advantage at home than in the thought of contributing seriously to the consideration and solution of the problems, they nevertheless correctly reflected the growing impatience of the Latin American peoples with their economically backward conditions, and their disillusionment with the high-sounding language of O.A.S. resolutions that failed to produce concrete economic benefits.

There is no doubt that the O.A.S. was intended to have a constructive role in this field. The Charter of Bogotá proclaimed it to be an essential purpose of the Organization to promote, by cooperative action, the economic, social, and cultural development of its member states. They likewise, in the same document, "agree to cooperate with one another, so far as their resources may permit and their laws may provide, in the broadest spirit of good neighborliness, in order to strengthen their economic structure, develop their agriculture and mining, promote their industry and increase their trade," as well as "to achieve just and decent living conditions for their entire populations." These and other laudable purposes had been restated and elaborated in countless resolutions and declarations. But, Latin Americans declared, there was little that could be pointed to in the way of concrete achievement comparable with the tangible and definite accomplishments in fulfillment of the purpose "to provide for common action . . . in the event of aggression."

There was considerable truth to these criticisms. The achievements of the O.A.S. in economic and social matters were limited largely to traditional forms of international cooperation in technical fields, through the specialized agencies and the various offices and services of the Pan American Union. While these activities within the limitations of their scope and resources were eminently worthwhile, and have some notable accomplishments to their credit, they still did not amount to a major contribution to the solution of basic economic and social problems in the Americas.

Just as the success of the O.A.S. in the field of peace and security can be explained by the happy coincidence of a number of forces and interests that contributed to a general desire to make the machinery work, there were powerful reasons for its relative ineffectiveness—one should not call it failure—in promoting economic and social betterment.

To understand the role of the O.A.S., it is first of all necessary to relate it to the over-all policy of the United States toward Latin America during the 1950s. The main objective of the United States in this period was to maintain maximum tranquility in the area. Preoccupied with the intensifying conflict with the Communist bloc in other parts of the world and called upon to invest vast amounts of manpower and treasure in containing Communist expansion, it was natural for the United States to consider the Latin American area—

fortunately remote from the scenes of conflict and virtually inaccessible to direct aggression—as relatively "safe." The less disturbance there was in the southern part of the continent, one might have said, the better would the United States be able to concentrate upon the critical situations involving direct conflict with the aggressive forces of the Communist bloc.

For this purpose, the strict observance of nonintervention and the maintenance of inter-American peace were highly suitable policies. Nonintervention relieved the United States of having to concern itself actively about the dictatorships or the internal social problems of the Latin American countries. Reliance upon the O.A.S. to maintain the peace was obviously the best way to prevent the worry of distracting conflicts and disturbances. While "crash programs" were devised to meet "crises" in other parts of the world, "normal" methods were generally considered suitable for the problems of Latin America. If reasonable political tranquility could prevail in the area, the traditional economic processes based upon private enterprise and normal trade (plus moderate public lending by the United States through the Export-Import Bank) would proceed to work, and in due course the Latin American countries would gradually climb up the ladder of economic development toward fuller employment, a respectable national income, social benefits, and political democracy.

That policy, it should be emphasized, was not a bad policy. It was based upon a sincere desire for friendship and cooperation. It involved definite governmental collaboration in the process of economic development through technical assistance programs and substantial public loans. It has been criticized as a policy of neglect of Latin America. But its major shortcoming was that it involved insufficient recognition of the increasingly urgent need to approach Latin America's long-standing problems in depth. Conservative formulas proved inadequate in a world that demanded imagination, creativity, and daring.

Quite apart from the conservatism of U.S. policy, there were other serious obstacles to the working out of effective programs of economic improvement on a regional basis, whether they involved trade, private investment, public loans, or technical assistance. These problems are likewise encountered in other regions of the world, and it is difficult for the United States to deal with them exclusively in a hemisphere context. The subject is well illustrated by so peculiarly Latin American a problem as coffee. The Latin American countries long wanted the United States to enter into a regional agreement, under the O.A.S. framework, to stabilize the coffee market; and such an agreement was in fact adopted during World War II, only to be abandoned thereafter. Yet any realistic effort to regulate the coffee market today, as has now been recognized, must take African producers into account, and European consumers as well.

In contemplating the use of the O.A.S. for economic development purposes, the United States must also resolve the knotty problem of the relative merits of a bilateral versus a multilateral approach. So long as the United States conducts its economic relations bilaterally with each Latin American government, it retains a maximum freedom of action and decision. But, once economic questions are submitted to an O.A.S. organ for decision, the United States becomes only one of twenty-one juridically equal members. To be sure, the Latin American members of the O.A.S. recognize that in most economic questions it is not so much what they say that counts as what the United States does. Mere majority votes cannot force the United States to do something that it is determined not to do. Yet the fact is—and the Latin Americans understand this well—that it is much harder for the United States, from the standpoint of public opinion and its political relations, to refuse a demand in which up to twenty Latin American countries unite under the floodlights of an international conference than it is to say a polite and private "no" to each of them separately.

To be sure, all twenty-one members of the regional organization have certain basic economic interests and objectives in common: the promotion of both regional and world trade, for example, or the raising of living standards in the Americas. But it is only to be expected that the immediate interests of the economically underdeveloped Latin American countries should often differ from, and sometimes conflict with, those of the economically advanced United States. The Latin American nations are sellers of raw materials; the United States is the main buyer. The former need foreign capital for development; the latter is the principal provider of it. They are borrowers, the United States the lender. There exists, therefore, a constant danger that, when it comes to economic affairs, the O.A.S. will degenerate into a simple pressure group wherein twenty Latin American countries seek to force their rich neighbor into accepting their demands. The question is whether it can serve as an instrument for reconciling interests so divergent.

Despite these problems, and the obvious reluctance of the United States over a long period of time to commit itself more vigorously to programs of economic assistance through the O.A.S., efforts to make more effective use of the Organization were made on many occasions. With their characteristically juridical approach to international problems, the Latin American countries repeatedly tried to get the United States to sign a treaty that would set forth the main policies to be followed by the United States and the other members of the O.A.S. in regard to all the principal problems of economic cooperation. In supporting this idea, to which the United States at no time gave any encouragement, the Latin American advocates of a treaty maintained that the happily successful example of the Treaty of Rio de Janeiro warranted adopting the same approach in the economic field.

The United States has not been averse to trying. Serious attempts to draft basic economic agreements or treaties were made on several occasions. At the Bogotá Conference in 1948 an agreement was drawn up, but it was subjected to so many reservations by so many governments that it proved completely useless. Several efforts to renegotiate it failed. The last great effort was at the Economic Conference of Buenos Aires in 1957, which likewise proved unable to resolve the long-standing policy conflicts on basic issues. Negotiations for comprehensive economic agreements in the O.A.S. have usually turned into sterile, doctrinaire debates on economic theory.

They have served only to widen, rather than to close, the breach between the United States and its neighbors in this area of their relations. It is to be hoped that the constructive steps of a very different character which are now being taken in the economic field will turn attention permanently from the highly unrealistic and futile proposition to set forth in one treaty the answers to all the economic problems of the hemisphere.

In addition to these fundamental reasons for the inability of the O.A.S. to perform more effectively in the economic and social field, there are others which flow from the nature of the O.A.S. agencies themselves. Their organization, their limited resources and their unproductive deliberations have reflected the very inadequacies and controversies which they were set up to help overcome.

The various inter-American conferences dealing with economic affairs between World War II and 1960 have rarely been productive. Incapable of surmounting the basic obstacles of conflicting policies in the more important areas of economic relations, they often served as little more than a public pillory in which the Latin American representatives would seek to extract some minor concessions from a harassed Uncle Sam by a process of political and oratorical torment. The experience hardly engendered any great enthusiasm in the United States for the holding of such conferences. In view of all these factors, it is not surprising that the Economic Conference of the O.A.S., first agreed upon in 1947, was in fact postponed time and again and not actually held until 1957.

Other O.A.S. bodies having principally to do with economic and social affairs are the Inter-American Economic and Social Council and the various Specialized Agencies. The Inter-American Economic and Social Council—known as IA-ECOSOC—is established in the Charter. Although set up as a subordinate organ of the Council of the O.A.S., the IA-ECOSOC was given, with more enthusiasm than practical foresight, a grandiose assignment it could not possibly fulfill. Article 63 of the Charter gives to this Council as "its principal purpose the promotion of the economic and social welfare of the American nations through effective cooperation for the better utilization of their natural resources, the development of their agriculture and industry and the raising of the standards of living of their peoples." Among the more specific functions is that of acting as "coordinating agency for all official inter-American activities of an economic and social nature."

The contrast is vivid between the rhetorically expressed ideal and the concrete reality of the IA-ECOSOC. Until its reorganization in 1961, it had little in the way of significant policy questions to consider. Important matters of economic relations were dealt with primarily through bilateral channels between the United States and the individual Latin American countries. Until very recently, the United States made little effort to use the IA-ECOSOC as a vehicle for the discussion and resolution of any significant questions. As a result, the other governments displayed little interest in it. They appointed as representatives members of their diplomatic missions in Washington who rarely had direct contact with the policy-level officials of their own governments in the economic field and therefore could hardly speak with real authority on questions of vital concern. The unproductiveness of the IA-ECOSOC further discouraged governments from drawing upon their all-too-scarce supply of expert personnel to staff their delegations. Lacking significant tasks, the IA-ECOSOC became more and more concerned with the minutiae of procedure and administration. Outside of its initiation and supervision of the O.A.S. Technical Cooperation Program and the preparation of studies on routine economic and social questions for consideration by various O.A.S. conferences, there was not much to which it could point by way of achievement.

As for the Specialized Agencies, with one exception they suffer from extreme limitations in budget and staff.[1] The same is true of the O.A.S. Technical Cooperation Program under the IA-ECOSOC,

---

[1] See pp. 35-36, above. These agencies and programs are for the most part financed under quota systems whereby the United States contributes from 66 to 70 per cent of the total. Many of the twenty Latin American governments often find it difficult to pay even the relatively small quotas which present budgets require of them.

which has established a number of important centers for the training of technical personnel in such fields as agriculture, housing statistics, and education. The concept is good, but the program's impact has been severely restricted by the limits of its financial resources.

Far more effective work on the economic and social problems of Latin America has, in fact, been done by United Nations agencies. The U.N.'s Economic Commission for Latin America (ECLA), endowed with a substantial budget and assembling a highly competent staff, produced a number of outstanding annual reports and special studies. It took the lead in promoting plans for Central American economic integration and the larger Latin American Free Trade Association, two of the most important initiatives in Latin America during the postwar period. ECLA's performance throughout the 1950s far outshone, in Latin American eyes, that of the meager economic staff of the O.A.S., not only for its scope and professional quality but also because of its sympathetic and in some respects unorthodox approach to the analysis of Latin America's economic position and requirements. The Latin American countries also benefited from membership in the International Bank for Reconstruction and Development and in the International Monetary Fund. Other United Nations agencies (notably the Food and Agriculture Organization, UNESCO, the Children's Emergency Fund, and the Program of Technical Cooperation) extended help to Latin America on a scale generally exceeding that of the O.A.S. From the standpoint of direct economic returns, membership in the United Nations proved to be a better investment for the Latin American countries than membership in the O.A.S. But for them the real question remained: what help, by whatever channels, would the United States provide?

As a result of the limitations on the capacity of the O.A.S. to act in the economic and social fields, efforts were made outside the existing formal organization to start something new. At the initiative of President Eisenhower the presidents of the American republics, meeting in Panama in 1956, established a committee of special representatives to consider how the O.A.S. might be used more effectively in furthering economic and social goals. The principal specific recommendations of this group that were carried out concerned the establishment of an O.A.S. scholarship program and the organization of an Inter-American Nuclear Energy Commission. It became clear by that time, however, that effective action by the O.A.S. required a more radical approach. A mere intensification of the small effort that was possible through the existing machinery was of minor usefulness. What was needed was a wholly new and reoriented program of inter-American economic and social cooperation cast in a larger mold and envisioning new methods of work.

## 2. *Operation Pan America to the Alliance for Progress*

This was the view taken by President Juscelino Kubitschek of Brazil when he launched what became known as "Operation Pan America." His position was that there had been enough "palliatives" to soothe the economic and social ills of the continent. What was necessary was a cure, and that would require a bolder and more ambitious approach than anything heretofore proposed. Significantly, Kubitschek's appeal had its political as well as its economic aspect. He spoke of the need for strengthening the solidarity of the American nations as a means of adding sinew and muscle to the whole fabric of Western civilization. As to the role of the Latin American countries, he emphasized that they wished to achieve a position of full partnership, and not to serve as an obedient chorus to be called upon to endorse views and positions in the formulation of which they had played no part.

No sooner had Operation Pan America been launched than it precipitated a heated controversy over the role, if any, of the O.A.S. in the projected programs of economic and social development. Mindful of the past deficiencies of the O.A.S. machinery, the Brazilians argued that the needs of inter-American economic and social cooperation far exceeded the scope and resources of the O.A.S.

and should be embodied in some new international institutions, free from the procedural and bureaucratic handicaps of the existing organs. Other governments, including the United States, feeling that this projected sidetracking of the regional organization would sound its death knell, insisted upon working within the framework of the O.A.S. At an informal meeting of foreign ministers, called by Secretary Dulles in Washington in September 1958, the issue was resolved by agreeing to set up a special Committee of the Council of the O.A.S. that became popularly known as the Committee of Twenty-one, for the purpose of devising the new measures of economic cooperation called for by Operation Pan America.

After the decision to proceed within the framework of the O.A.S., there followed in rapid succession several steps to revise the machinery of the Organization in order to enable it to deal adequately with these larger problems. The first was the creation within the Inter-American System of a new agency: the Inter-American Development Bank. Announcement by the United States that it was ready to make an about-face in its policy and to support the establishment of an inter-American lending institution came as a bombshell in the O.A.S. The revelation of the new policy at a hastily called meeting of the Inter-American Economic and Social Council was in part dictated by President Eisenhower's then imminent proposal to set up an international lending agency for the Middle East under the aegis of the United Nations—a step that would have highlighted the relative inattention to the needs of the American region. More importantly, however, the new policy reflected the growing awareness of the United States that more positive attention to the economic problems of the hemisphere was now indispensable, and that new programs of economic aid should be cast in a multilateral mold, tailored to the needs of the region.

The charter of the new bank, which draws upon various international precedents,[2] constitutes a significant innovation in inter-

[2] In 1940 a convention establishing an Inter-American Bank was actually signed by the United States, but did not receive the necessary approval of the Senate for ratification. The convention never became effective, being ratified only by Mexico.

American organization, especially in voting procedure. Decisions are reached by a system of weighted voting, based in part upon the sovereign equality of the member states but in part also upon their relative contributions to the total capital subscribed. As the major subscriber, the United States has a large voice, but not a veto, in decisions regarding the Bank's use of its regular funds. Decisions to grant loans require the concurrence of a majority of the votes of the Latin American directors. A satisfactory formula has thus been developed whereby the United States shares with the other members of the O.A.S. the responsibility for determining how and to whom the funds, to which the United States had made the largest contribution, should be made available for the economic and social progress of the hemisphere community.

Another recent step of importance has been the reorganization of the IA-ECOSOC, an objective vainly sought at numerous earlier inter-American conferences. Under the influence of the new approach to hemisphere economic relations, the American governments have decided to streamline the economic council and free it from its past preoccupation with unimportant detail. Henceforth the IA-ECOSOC will meet only twice yearly: once on the expert level and once on the ministerial level. It will concentrate its efforts on an annual review of the progress made by the member governments toward the achievement of their goals in economic and social development. A larger and better qualified staff in the economic and social departments of the Pan American Union will, under this arrangement, enjoy a greater opportunity to carry out constructive professional tasks. Moreover, a new and closer collaboration between IA-ECOSOC on the one hand and ECLA on the other will result in a transfer of some of the latter's functions to the former and better all-round coordination of the work of these two multilateral agencies.

The organizational improvements in the inter-American system in the period 1959-61 reflected a change in policy on the part of the United States that is of major significance. It may well prove to be of equal importance to the historic change that took place in the early 1930s with respect to the issue of nonintervention. First of all, the United States has accepted a larger and broader commitment to cooperate for the economic and social development of the Latin American countries, thus responding to repeated appeals from its hemisphere neighbors. Secondly—and most important from the standpoint of the O.A.S.—the United States has agreed to fulfill a large part of this commitment through the multilateral machinery of the Inter-American System. Like the earlier change that ushered in the nonintervention period, the new policy of the United States developed gradually and on a nonpartisan basis, covering the transition from a Republican to a Democratic administration.

A major indication of the acceptance by the United States of a greater responsibility for the collective welfare of the hemisphere came at the meeting of the Committee of Twenty-one at Bogotá in September 1960, when C. Douglas Dillon, then Under Secretary of State in the Eisenhower administration, called for a fresh approach to the social as well as economic problems of the Americas. He pledged a sum of $500 million from the United States, over and above the amounts already made available, to help initiate a broad program aiming at the fundamental social problems: land reform, health, housing, and education. Such a program was adopted in the Act of Bogotá which emerged from the conference. The new policy was subsequently broadened and vitalized by President Kennedy in his speech of March 13, 1961, proclaiming an Alliance for Progress among the American nations and calling for the formulation of a ten-year program of economic and social development. To this end, a special meeting of IA-ECOSOC on the ministerial level, was held in August 1961 at Punta del Este, Uruguay, to draft the concrete terms of the program and specify the measures to put it into practice.

The Alliance for Progress, which will be considered more fully later on, projects not only intensified bilateral measures of economic and social cooperation but also greatly increased activity through the Inter-American Development Bank, the Pan American Union, and the Inter-American Economic and Social Council. The O.A.S., therefore, now stands ready for the first time in its history to participate significantly in a broad attack upon the basic economic and social problems of the hemisphere. In so doing, it will encounter some of the most complex difficulties and pressing demands that the American republics and the organized inter-American community have ever faced. These are the problems posed by the tide of social revolution that is now sweeping through Latin America.

# V

# The Impact
# of Social Revolution

*1. "Pan, Tierra y Libertad"*

Like many historic movements, the social revolution in Latin America is fundamentally simple in broad outline and highly complex in detail. Its objectives are political as well as economic and social, with implications for both the national and international scene. To gain a perspective upon these objectives one has but to contrast what the deeper popular movements in Latin America are seeking today with the pattern of political, economic, and social organization that has existed traditionally.

The traditional pattern of society that developed in Latin America during the colonial period and early nineteenth century, although subject to many variations in detail and despite some basic alterations achieved by the forces of modernization in many countries, was essentially the following. Land—and this meant property in general—was held in large estates deriving from grants made by the Spanish or Portuguese crown and covering not only the land itself but the population living on it. Peonage was the common lot of the peasants, especially among the indigenous peoples who in many areas made up the majority of the population. The Roman Catholic

Church in that period generally buttressed the system of social control by what has often been called a land-owning and military oligarchy, though exercising a moderating influence over some of its harsher manifestations. Government rested essentially upon military power, although the forms of democracy were often used as a façade to cover the naked force which manipulated elections and made a mockery of constitutions. Political power was at best confined to the hands of the oligarchy and all too frequently, both on the provincial and national level, was seized by a *caudillo*—a dictator who ruled through varying combinations of political acumen and brute force.

To complete the broad outlines of the picture, one more element must be added to the landowner, the church, and the military chieftain: the foreign investor. The *caudillos* considered the land their own private domain, available for their personal exploitation. (A recent example of this, archaic in our own time, was the Dominican Republic, where the late Generalissimo Trujillo converted virtually the whole country into his family estate.) To realize the potentialities of their resources, the *caudillos* or oligarchies often turned to foreign investors and made them attractive concessions in land grants, tax exemptions, and monopolies. In many cases dictators provided the political and economic stability that foreign venture capital sought; foreign capital in turn provided the cash that the oligarchy desired, much of which was diverted into the pockets of the ruling authorities in the form of graft.

Since the foreign investor was in most cases from the United States (although British and other European capital was predominant in some countries), there developed in many instances what appeared in Latin American eyes to be a working arrangement between oppressive governments and U.S. economic interests. Not that this result was sought per se, or in recent years even considered desirable, by responsible representatives of U.S. business. But during the nineteenth century, and in many countries far into the twentieth, there was no alternative to tying up with the powers-that-were if one wanted to do business. That fact did not alter the basic impression made upon the Latin American peoples, who often overlooked the very real economic benefits involved and saw in the situation only a combination of economic exploitation and political suppression.

Like any generalization, this one has its shortcomings. Yet like any good generalization it contains, too, a touch of illuminating truth. The situation described in the foregoing paragraphs was essentially that which prevailed in Mexico in 1910, when the dictatorship of General Porfirio Díaz crumbled in the longest, bloodiest, and most drastic revolution that Latin America has ever experienced. It was the situation that dominated the history of Venezuela, except for brief intervals, until the present regime of President Rómulo Betancourt. It was, with many modifications, still the basic pattern against which Cuban democrats had struggled since their liberation from Spain, and which had returned with force under Batista. Aspects of the traditional order persist in one degree or another in all the Latin American countries—even in those where its worst features have been eliminated by violence, as in Mexico, or by political evolution, as in Uruguay or Chile.

The social revolution in Latin America is in part the result of the fact that the people have now sufficiently awakened to the realization that this age-old pattern of exploitation and suppression, wherever it still exists, not only should but can be destroyed. For rule by *caudillo* and oligarchy, popular movements wish to substitute governments that will respect human rights and be responsive to the people's demands. For monopolistic landownership and a landless peasantry, they want to substitute a more equitable distribution of land and greater security for the farm worker. For foreign domination of their economies—real or imagined—they want to substitute national control over all economic enterprise in order to assure its development in the public interest. Closely associated with the latter purpose is the desire among nationalist groups to assert a greater independence and freedom of action in the international sphere, and especially to remove any stigma of subordination to the foreign policy of the United States. The achievement of major economic and social reforms, the raising of living standards, and the assurance of political liberties are now the great tasks facing the inter-American community. And as the traditional order crumbles, another task assumes major importance: the protection of the Latin American social revolution and its democratic character from penetration and subversion by Communist forces subservient to Moscow or Peking. All these problems have come to a focus in the case of Cuba.

Latin Americans of virtually all classes hailed the Castro revolution when it overthrew the Batista dictatorship in 1959, and welcomed the promises of honest and democratic government that came from Castro's lips. The vast majority applauded his seizure of large landholdings and his announced intention to make agrarian reform a major feature of his new state. His programs to improve the material welfare of the rural and urban workers evoked echoes of similar demands, and therefore enthusiastic approval, on the part of the masses in other Latin American countries. Finally, his open break with the United States, while it created concern among the more sober-minded groups and individuals in Latin America, also met with an emotionally sympathetic response. For here was the brave leader of a small country openly defying the greatest power on earth. In virtually all respects, the Castro revolution at its beginning responded to the deepest aspirations of the peoples of all Latin America.

As time went on, and the character of the Cuban revolution changed, the enthusiasm began to be tempered with serious worry. Sincere democrats deplored the shooting of political prisoners, the failure to hold elections, and the conversion of a popular democratic movement into a dictatorship which, like those of the past, turned out to be nothing more than one-man rule. Strong opposition was expressed to Castro's increasingly open association with the Communists both domestically and internationally. But none of these disturbing factors—and no combination of them—was strong enough to change the fundamental attitude of tolerance, if not encouragement, toward the Cuban revolution itself. Mexicans could, and did, point out that it took them seven years from the start of their revolution to hold an election. Moreover, violence is unfortunately all too common a phenomenon in Latin American politics. And, so long as the revolutionary government of Cuba did not formally align itself with the Soviet bloc or denounce the treaties that bound it to the O.A.S., the predominant opinion in Latin America was infused with the hope and even expectation that, with the passage of time and the settlement of its disputes with the United States, Cuba would keep its place as a member of the inter-American community.

For many Latin Americans who deeply disapproved of some of Castro's policies it was still a cause of satisfaction that he and his regime existed. He personified a heroic breakthrough in the struggle to achieve some of their most deeply felt desires. How could they then bring themselves to take the side of the "Colossus of the North" against this heroic figure of Latin America? Castro well knew that his greatest defense was to proclaim and provoke the opposition, both real and imagined, of the United States to his revolution, thus gaining sympathy and friendship throughout Latin America and preventing less radical figures in other countries from taking positions against him which their sober judgment recommended.

To support action by the O.A.S. against Cuba in the early period after Castro took power would have been, in the eyes of most Latin Americans, to use the Organization for a purpose directly contrary to one of its most elemental functions: the protection of the small Latin American countries against the intervention of the United States. Sanctions of any kind against Cuba, they feared, would threaten the very existence of the nonintervention principle upon which the freedom and self-determination of Latin America rested. And in the event that Castro were overthrown as a result of U.S. pressure and O.A.S. approval, who would take his place? What would happen to the movement for fundamental change and reform, not only in Cuba but in other countries which aspired to similar achievements? Would U.S. interests, backed by the big landowners and local industrialists, seek to re-establish the traditional pattern of political, economic, and social institutions? These were not the views of the extreme left only. For a long time these questions burned fiercely in the minds of many others when the United States brought up the question of O.A.S. action to deal with what had become a

Communist intrusion in the hemisphere. That the United States proceeded in measured terms and against a background of considerable patience and self-restraint did not seem to make any difference.

Most Latin American political leaders, focusing their attention upon the possible danger of intervention by the United States, at first underestimated, or perhaps did not wish to see, the actual danger of Communist infiltration in Cuba, and through Cuba in other countries of the continent. In effect, in the two conferences at Santiago in 1959 and at San José in 1960, and on other occasions when the issue of O.A.S. action was raised, the Latin Americans did what John Foster Dulles had referred to at the Caracas Conference as "incredible": they preferred "that the American states should leave themselves exposed to international communism rather than run the risk that the doctrine of collective security might be turned by American states themselves into a doctrine of collective intervention." [1] Even the subsequent removal of all basis for doubt, by virtue of Castro's own confession of Marxist-Leninist faith in December 1961, did not eliminate, though it reduced, the opposition to O.A.S. action.

It was, however, not only the fear of violating the principle of nonintervention that contributed to the rigid reluctance of the Latin American governments to act through the O.A.S. on the issue of communism in Cuba. It was also the fear of seeming to take sides against a popular revolutionary movement that enjoyed widespread sympathy in all the other countries. This fear was magnified by the extreme form of the anti-Communist position expressed by the U.S. government and many prominent American citizens on several occasions, and by the fact that the most unsavory dictatorial regimes in Latin America had rallied to the anti-Communist standard in the past. It was widely recognized that Batista, Trujillo, and Pérez Jiménez, to mention only three notorious dictators, had earned favor in the United States because of their firm anticommunism. Rightly or wrongly, the Guatemalan episode and other aspects of

---

[1] *Tenth Inter-American Conference, Caracas, Venezuela, March 1-28, 1954,* Report of the Delegation of the United States of America, Department of State Publication 5692 (Washington: GPO, 1955), p. 62.

U.S. policy in the past had tarnished the standing of the United States as a true friend of democracy among many Latin Americans.

Thus, the seeming readiness of the United States at times to sacrifice other positive considerations—which may be of major importance to other nations—to the one factor of anticommunism augmented the already excessive sensitivity of Latin Americans to any suggestion of intervention in Cuba. In their own countries, they had seen many fall victims to an anticommunism that was in reality nothing but a cloak for plain, old-fashioned dictatorship. They did not wish the same slogan to serve as an excuse to extinguish the gains of social revolution in Cuba or anywhere else. Even where the leaders of government were able to perceive the nature of the Cuban problem more realistically, the fact that few of their citizens did likewise made governments reluctant to take action against Castro for fear of strengthening political opposition at home.

With these emotional considerations in full play, it was obvious that the O.A.S. would not easily decide to take action on the Cuban problem as sought by the United States. Respectable argument against such action was not lacking. The principle of nonintervention is always a profitable platform on which to appeal to Latin American opinion. Moreover, as our review of the nature and powers of the organs of the O.A.S. has shown, there are checks and restraints on all sides. It is no trouble at all to find any number of juridical objections to positive action once a sufficient emotional reluctance is engendered.

Does the experience of the past three years with regard to Cuba mean, then, that the O.A.S. is a useless instrument for dealing with the danger of Communist subversion of Latin America's social revolution and the extension of extracontinental Communist control over whole countries in this hemisphere? Opinion in the United States often tends to measure the validity of the O.A.S. and the Inter-American System today in those terms. Similar, though less pointed, concern on this score is also felt in many circles in Latin America. Before rendering a judgment on this point, we should examine a little further what is involved, and see what criteria are most important from the standpoint of Latin American opinion.

The validity of the O.A.S. and of its associated body of political and juridical principles is most likely to be judged in Latin American opinion by their ability to contribute to the achievement of the major goals that evoke so powerful a response among the peoples of those countries at this time: the improvement of economic and social conditions and the development of governments duly responsive to the popular will. We have seen that the historical record of the Organization in these respects leaves much to be desired. If, as a result of recent steps, the O.A.S. can be prominently associated in the eyes of the Latin American peoples with active progress toward these goals, then, and only then, can it be expected that they will have sufficient confidence in the Organization to support firm measures through it to cope effectively with the problems of Communist subversion.

The answer to the question posed above, therefore, is not likely to be immediate or clear-cut. This is evidenced by the boggling attitude still displayed by some of the major member governments of the O.A.S. as recently as the Eighth Meeting of Consultation of Ministers of Foreign Affairs held at Punta del Este in January 1962. Although the resolution declaring the Castro regime "incompatible" with the Inter-American System was carried unanimously, the paragraph excluding Cuba from the Inter-American System received only a bare two-thirds majority, with six Latin American countries (including Argentina, Brazil, Chile, and Mexico) abstaining. The answer will ultimately depend a great deal on the performance of the O.A.S. in both the political and the economic field during the coming months and years. Let us consider some of the main problems the O.A.S. faces in this respect, and what a successful performance on its part will demand of it.

## 2. Encouragement of Political Democracy

Some indication of the nature of the political problems can be gained from the experience of the O.A.S. in its efforts to contribute to the strengthening of democracy and respect for human rights in

Latin America, and the ensuing conflict with the strict nonintervention principle. This conflict was clearly delineated in 1945 by a proposal of the Uruguayan Foreign Minister, Eduardo Rodríguez Larreta. He advanced the proposition that the strict adherence to the principle of nonintervention should not be permitted to protect the notorious and repeated violation of other accepted inter-American principles, particularly basic human rights. Stressing the relationship between peace and democracy, Dr. Rodríguez Larreta suggested that action by the community of American states to protect human rights and democracy was justified and juridically acceptable as a step to maintain international peace. He proposed consultation among the American governments to decide how to do it.

Dr. Rodríguez Larreta's thesis was decisively rejected by the majority of the American governments. The United States was one of eight which accepted it and expressed a willingness to consult with a view to further steps. The others displayed a firm resolve to prevent any weakening in the principle of nonintervention, even on the grounds that intervention might be necessary in the interests of inter-American peace. The potential dangers inherent in permitting any kind of intervention were considered greater than the evils which intervention under the Rodríguez Larreta doctrine was intended to correct. A similar rejection was accorded the thesis advanced by Guatemala in 1945 that recognition should be withheld from governments established by force until free elections had confirmed their popular support.

The issue, however, has not disappeared. Indeed, the entire question of promoting democracy and respect for human rights through the O.A.S. assumes a greater significance and urgency today than it had before, for the development of political institutions that will assure a respect for the essential rights of man is intimately associated with the ends of the social revolution. The vigorous support of democratic principles, moreover, constitutes the most effective political weapon with which to combat Communist efforts to subvert the revolutionary processes and seize political power. A predominantly negative approach confined to anticommunism has already demonstrated its inadequacy and ineffectiveness. A positive espousal of democratic principles and respect for human rights is clearly necessary.

No one familiar with the political history of Latin America will fail to appreciate the profound difficulties to be overcome before democratic processes can be made effective. It is even open to question whether representative democracy as it is known in the United States and most of Western Europe can flourish throughout a group of countries displaying such varied conditions of population, education, economic and social progress, and political development as do those of Latin America. Most of them, in contrast to the United States, have had little constructive experience with representative institutions. Many of the apparent forms of democracy that they have had, including constitutions and electoral systems, are actually misleading or without substance. Imported largely from the United States and Western Europe, these institutions were grafted on societies that were in many respects not ready for them and could not make them work. In some countries, particularly those where European stock predominated and large-scale immigration from Europe during the early twentieth century had created a politically more experienced populace, considerable success has attended the persistent efforts to establish political democracy. In others, the firm grip of the traditional semi-feudal system of political and social control, and the wide gulf between rulers and ruled, effectively prevented anything but lip service to democratic ideals. Even in countries which have experienced deep social revolutions, representative democracy has not followed automatically in its train. Mexico's now fifty-year-old political system shows its own unique forms of democracy within a one-party system; while Bolivia, beset with the violent repercussions of her revolution, is still a long way from establishing a firm, democratic regime. Cuba is following the totalitarian path.

The call for action through the O.A.S. to strengthen democracy in the hemisphere is presented in two different forms. One type of action has to do with specific situations involving the notorious suppression of democratic liberties and human rights. The other type of action is more general in application: that of devising rules, procedures, and policies to help the forward march of democracy and respect for human rights in all countries and at a more gradual, evolutionary pace. Action of both kinds has been stimulated by the doings of the Castro regime during the past three years.

The Cuban revolutionary movement, at first openly dedicated to the promotion of democracy, made little effort to hide its efforts to overthrow governments it called dictatorships in other countries. In time it became clear that the Castro regime was serving as the vanguard not of democracy but of Communist expansion, and that it sought the downfall of the most democratic governments in the Caribbean region as well as those that were less notable in that respect. Although his revolution still has a great appeal throughout Latin America, Castro's open challenge to democracy, his frank espousal of Marxism-Leninism, his creation of an authoritarian militia-state wherein the Communist party rules alone, and his blatant disregard of political rights and freedoms have also stimulated a more vigorous reaction on behalf of representative democracy and respect for human rights in other countries. This has been particularly notable on the part of labor leaders, some student organizations, and other liberal and left-wing groups among whom Castro formerly found much support. It was also true that some Latin American governments, especially the more democratic ones, were as much or more exercised about dictatorships of the right, like Trujillo's in the Dominican Republic, than they were about Cuba.

The Dominican Republic provides an example of the kind of specific problem which the O.A.S. cannot evade. Ruled until May 1961 by the most absolute, ruthless, and hated dictator in the hemisphere, the Dominican Republic symbolized all that was diseased in the pathology of Latin American politics. It became clear that no collective action in regard to the growing Communist menace in Cuba could be achieved through the O.A.S. unless and until some effective action were taken to demonstrate that the inter-American community was at least as gravely concerned over the violation of human rights and denial of democracy by a native dictator as it was over the oppressive character of a revolutionary regime which, though a Communist-type police state, had a social program appealing to so many people in Latin America.

The United States had long maintained a cool but formally correct posture toward the government of Generalissimo Trujillo, avoiding action that could be interpreted as intervention in Dominican affairs. We had been widely accused in Latin America of supporting the Trujillo dictatorship because of its strong anticommunist policy. But beginning at the Fifth Meeting of Consultation of Ministers of Foreign Affairs at Santiago in 1959, the United States began to adopt a more positive position toward democracy in Latin America and to display a harder attitude toward dictatorships of all kinds. The changed mood of the United States was to a considerable degree responsible for the strong criticisms of dictatorship in general, and of the Dominican government in particular, that were voiced by the Inter-American Peace Committee in some of its reports on Caribbean problems. Then came the charge by Venezuela that the Dominican government had been involved in the plot to assassinate President Rómulo Betancourt. At the Sixth Meeting of Foreign Ministers at San José in 1960, the members of the O.A.S. were put to the test in regard to their willingness to take measures through the Organization that would substantially alter the internal political situation in the Dominican Republic.

The specific charge against the Dominican government, supported by evidence collected by the O.A.S. Council's Investigating Committee, was, to be sure, not that it was a cruel dictatorship, but that it had committed an act of aggression against Venezuela. However, the act in question—the attempted assassination—was long since past, and there was no evidence to indicate that further aggressive acts were then being planned by the Dominican government. The adoption by the Meeting of Foreign Ministers of sanctions against the Dominican Republic could, therefore, have only two purposes: either to punish the Dominican government for its past crime; or to bring about a fundamental change in the government, on the grounds that so long as Trujillo remained in power he would inevitably keep international relations in the area in a state of turmoil and tension.

It was apparent that the O.A.S. had in the Dominican case an ideal opportunity to take action in support of democratic principles and human rights as a measure needed to maintain peace and security. The Inter-American Peace Committee had stated that "international tensions in the Caribbean region have been aggravated by flagrant and widespread violations of human rights . . . in the Dominican Republic," and that "these tensions will continue to increase so long as the flagrant violations of human rights in the Dominican Republic persists." [2] The Dominican government had committed an act that justified the invocation of the Treaty of Rio de Janeiro and the imposition of its sanctions. What more reasonable than to take action that would eliminate the situation which, in the words of an O.A.S. organ itself, was responsible for the international tensions of which this reprehensible deed was but one manifestation?

There was no doubt at the San José Meeting of Foreign Ministers that most of the governments saw things that way and felt that now was the chance for the O.A.S. to take a historic step toward ridding the inter-American community of one of its most hated despots. Yet to do so would be to assume a great responsibility for developments in the Dominican Republic if the dictator were eliminated. The situation brought forcibly into relief the fact, so easily overlooked, that to get rid of a despot is not to establish democracy. How could one be sure that if the Generalissimo, who had ruled the island republic for over thirty years, were suddenly removed, his power would not fall into the hands of the rising young ruler, equally despotic, from the neighboring island republic of Cuba? Thus, to assure the establishment of a democratic government in the Dominican Republic would require a whole train of measures for which the O.A.S. would have to assume responsibility. This was made clear at San José by

[2] Inter-American Peace Committee, *Report of the Inter-American Peace Committee on the Case Presented by Venezuela* (Washington: Pan American Union, June 7, 1960; mimeographed).

Secretary of State Herter, who suggested that, instead of immediately applying sanctions against the Dominican Republic, the O.A.S. attempt to get the Dominican government to accept a committee which, as he explained later, would "be fully empowered to assure that free elections were held under its supervision." This power, it became clear, would involve far more than merely observing the casting of ballots: the O.A.S. group would virtually have to take control over the political machinery of the Dominican state and superintend the relaxation of police terror, the establishment of political parties, and the conduct of electoral campaigns under proper safeguards.

The proposal shocked many of the other governments: here was a frank suggestion that the O.A.S. intervene in the internal political affairs of a member state to a degree never before dreamed of. The nonintervention principle was invoked in opposition, and the proposal for a committee to supervise elections received little support. The Meeting of Foreign Ministers voted instead to break diplomatic relations and to interrupt economic relations, beginning with the suspension of trade in arms and implements of war. It was a drastic and unprecedented action nonetheless.

The Dominican problem was not, of course, solved by the O.A.S. either at San José or thereafter. The end came by violence to Rafael Leonidas Trujillo Molina, as it has to many others who ruled by violence. In the cautious action taken through the Council of the O.A.S. after the assassination of the dictator, there was little willingness to stretch the rigid principle of nonintervention in the interest of assuring that definite steps toward the establishment of a democratic regime would be taken; and little assurance that the Dominican Republic would not drift into chaos, Castroism, or another military dictatorship. To be sure, the sanctions imposed by the decision of the San José meeting prior to Trujillo's death were used thereafter as a lever to encourage the democratization of the subsequent regime. And a significant precedent was set by the sending of an O.A.S. technical assistance mission to advise the new government on the establishment of its electoral system. The political situation deteriorated, however, to the point where it called for a larger measure of firmness than the O.A.S. was prepared to provide. It apparently took a show of force by the United States to prevent a return to power of the Trujillo family, and the good offices of some skillful diplomats working outside of the O.A.S. to induce a settlement among the competing Dominican political groups. The result was to open the way at least to the initial establishment of democratic, constitutional government.

Now that the sanctions imposed by the O.A.S. in 1960 have been lifted, we can only hope that the inevitable political tensions and rivalries of the future will not vitiate the steps taken so far, through and outside the O.A.S., to help the Dominican people progress toward a government based on the democracy and respect for human rights that were so long denied them.

Meanwhile, the O.A.S. has also wrestled with a more general approach to promoting greater respect for democratic processes. The recent efforts to revive O.A.S. action in this field likewise were initiated at the Santiago Meeting of Foreign Ministers in 1959, when the conflict between promotion of democracy and nonintervention was met, discussed, and left unresolved. A major obstacle encountered by some of the more vociferous proponents of O.A.S. action to punish a government guilty of antidemocratic conduct was the absence, contrary to some assertions, of any treaty obligation among the American republics to observe any specific form or rule of democracy. General declarations of adherence to democracy as an aspiration, or goal, abound. The most notable is Article 5 (d) of the O.A.S. Charter itself, stating that the high aims of inter-American solidarity require the organization of the member states on the basis of the effective exercise of representative democracy. But no treaty obligation to put that noble thought into practice exists. There was therefore adopted at Santiago a resolution recommending the drafting of a convention under which states would bind themselves to observe certain democratic procedures and to apply sanctions against a party which was found to have violated the pledge. This highly idealistic project has been debated at length in one of the committees of the Council of the O.A.S. At this juncture there is no serious prospect of its being actually drafted, let alone adopted and put into effect.

A more practical approach is represented by two proposals that have been put forward to enable the O.A.S. to assist member governments in perfecting their electoral machinery and holding fair elections. Nicaragua proposed that the Council should respond favorably to requests that it designate observers for national elections; this was President Luis Somoza's answer to the critics who claimed he was planning to perpetuate his family's personal rule in the elections scheduled for 1963. The other proposal came from the United States. It urged that the Inter-American Human Rights Commission develop a plan whereby the O.A.S. might, on request of member governments, give technical help in planning and carrying out elections in order to assure their fair and free character.

Both these proposals are now technically under study by the Council, having been referred to that body by the Meeting of Foreign Ministers. The fact that no positive action has been taken upon them is indicative of the problems facing the Council in such matters. Two main obstacles must be overcome before any favorable decision to have the O.A.S. play a role in elections is reached. One is the understandable fear that the O.A.S. may well be used as a whitewash for fraudulent elections staged by clever politicians in control of governmental machinery. Such an obstacle would appear to be superable by means of adequate safeguards in the procedure to be followed. The other and principal obstacle is the old bogey of nonintervention, which here again stands in the way of the performance by the O.A.S. of a function of major importance to the political progress of the hemisphere. It can hardly be overcome until Latin America has governments whose real desire for more democratic practices weighs more heavily in the balance than their fear of international guarantees and procedures needed to bring it about.

There appears little likelihood for the present, therefore, that the O.A.S. will assume a significant role in the encouragement of democratic practices in individual countries. The major accomplishment of the regional organization in this field remains a doctrinal one: the clarification of what, among the member states, is understood by the term "representative democracy." This constituted the substance of the Declaration of Santiago, adopted at the Fifth Meeting of Foreign Ministers, in which there are set forth eight "principles and attributes of the democratic system in this hemisphere," including such basic elements as free elections, the separation of powers, and freedom of expression. With this declaration the generalizations about democracy have at least become a little less general.

### 3. Protection of Human Rights

Concurrently with efforts to further democratic aims among the American states, the governments through the O.A.S. are pursuing a closely related objective, the respect for human rights. The American Declaration of the Rights and Duties of Man, adopted at the Bogotá Conference in 1948, was the first international declaration of human rights to be approved, antedating the United Nations Declaration of Human Rights by a few months. Human rights, like the promotion of democracy, were relegated to an inferior position in the O.A.S. program during the era of absolute nonintervention, but likewise received a new stimulus following the Cuban revolution.

The Santiago Meeting of Foreign Ministers gave a boost to a project already under way for the drafting of an inter-American convention on human rights. Such a document was prepared shortly after the Santiago meeting by the Inter-American Council of Jurists for submission to the Eleventh Inter-American Conference to be held in Quito. Modeled after the European convention of similar nature, the draft convention sets forth the basic rights to be protected, then establishes a judicial procedure for the consideration of individual complaints against governments for violations of human rights. It would, if adopted, be a forward step of considerable magnitude for the O.A.S. At present it rests in the limbo of uncertainty created by the indefinite postponement of the Eleventh Inter-American Conference.

Not content with this long-range plan based upon a convention, the Santiago Meeting of Foreign Ministers also proceeded to set up (by Resolution 8) another Inter-American Commission on Human Rights "charged with furthering respect for such rights." The Commission was to be organized by the Council of the O.A.S. and to have "the specific functions that the Council assigns to it." Having received this vaguely formulated assignment, the Council proceeded to draft a statute outlining the nature and competence of the Commission. Eight months were consumed in this task, with lines rather sharply drawn on the fundamental issue of whether the Commission should have the right to consider individual cases of complaints involving the violation of human rights, or should be restricted to the kind of general educational and promotional work that is carried on by the United Nations Human Rights Commission. Exponents of nonintervention won out in the end, and the Commission's power to consider individual cases was excluded from the final statute.

In a reversal of usual roles, the leadership of the nonintervention forces on this issue passed from the more familiar hands of Mexico to those of the United States. Mexico joined several other Latin American countries in favoring the delegation of authority to the Commission to review and take limited action on certain kinds of complaints by individual persons against governments. The United States opposed this authority on both legal and political grounds. It maintained that such authority to intervene in the internal affairs of member states could only be given to an O.A.S. organ by means of a treaty, which the statute was not intended to be; and furthermore, that any attempt to investigate complaints of violations of human rights in member states was unwise in the absence of any inter-American or international agreement as to the precise nature of the rights that were to be protected. This uncertainty, it was held, would make of the Commission a scene of political maneuverings and contribute more to the creation of inter-American tensions than to the protection of human rights.

These views of the United States, ultimately backed by some of the larger South American countries, prevailed. Yet the battle is not yet over. At its first and second meetings, the Commission, with the single dissent of the U.S. member, urged the governments to modify the statute in order that it might have the power to do something in regard to individual cases and avoid being confined to its present theoretical and academic function. At Punta del Este, in 1962, the Foreign Ministers agreed that the Commission should be strengthened. The subject is therefore again under consideration in the Council.

## 4. Economic and Social Change

A challenge of equal magnitude and greater urgency is presented to the O.A.S. as it moves into the field of economic and social development. The program which the American states have set out for themselves in the broad sweep of the Act of Bogotá (1960) and the Alliance for Progress is unprecedented in inter-American affairs. Previous efforts to resolve economic questions, whether bilateral or multilateral, had been of only limited scope and depth. As a result of the steps taken in the past two years there has now been launched a comprehensive and fundamental effort to eliminate the main obstructions to economic and social progress. The purpose is not merely to engage in useful activity that will help here and there: it is to set in motion a fundamental change for the better in the whole structure of Latin America's economic and social institutions.

Perhaps the most significant development in the consideration of economic and social problems in the O.A.S. was the frank recognition in the Act of Bogotá of the complexity of the problem that the Latin American countries face in attempting to reach the goal of increased productivity and higher living standards. For years the United States had emphasized to the Latin Americans the need to follow sound economic policies and take drastic, if unpleasant, measures to set their own houses in order if they wished to profit by foreign aid. For years the Latin Americans had tended to maintain that their principal needs were better prices for their products and larger public loans, and that it was up to the United States to make them available. In the Act of Bogotá both sides finally agreed on the need for a joint attack on all phases of economic and social development and recognized that drastic changes in the internal policies and institutions of the Latin American countries must be made.

In outlining the main features of the new inter-American program of social development, the Act of Bogotá speaks of the need "to modernize and improve the existing legal and institutional framework to ensure better conditions of land tenure, extend more adequate credit facilities and provide increased incentives in the land tax structure." This is seen as essential to the achievement of the broader program of improving the conditions of rural life and agriculture generally. Housing is another primary requirement, calling for new laws, new institutions, and a vastly expanded effort. Improvement and strengthening of health and educational systems in all countries constitute another main segment of the proposed program. Finally, recognizing the need for the better "mobilization of domestic resources" including "the maximum creation of domestic savings" and the "improvement of fiscal and financial practices," the Act of Bogotá calls for a re-examination of "the equity and effectiveness of existing tax schedules, assessment practices and collection procedures," in order to provide additional revenue to the governments for the broad program envisaged in the social field.

Couched in soft, somewhat vague terms, these statements nevertheless carry an impact and implication of historic importance. For they say, in effect, that the program of inter-American social development—and the economic progress which in turn depends on it—requires a frontal attack on the most deeply entrenched privileges in the Latin American social scene. Agrarian reform, whether it means heavy taxation of unused land, purchase and redistribution of large holdings, or improved social conditions for the *campesinos*, strikes at the interests of the oligarchies that have occupied a ruling position in most Latin American countries since the days of the conquistadors. Less obvious, but no less strategic, are the interests that would be affected by a modernization of tax systems resulting in higher taxes and more effective collection procedures. Strong opposition, therefore, may be expected from those interests adversely affected by the inexorable requirements of social progress. Inertia obstructs progress in other fields where personal interests are not so directly affected—as, for example, in the creation of savings and loan institutions, and adequate educational and health programs. A broad and continual pressure for change, in lands where change has been traditionally resisted, is sought in this almost revolutionary pronouncement of the members of the O.A.S. Will they exert it?

Frank recognition of the need for this change as an essential ingredient in any successful use of U.S. funds for economic and social development in Latin America was voiced by President Kennedy, both in his memorable speech to the Latin American diplomatic corps of March 13, 1961, and his message to the Congress on the following day. Speaking of the social development program accepted at Bogotá, he said: "Its effectiveness depends on the willingness of each recipient nation to improve its own institutions, make necessary modifications in its own social patterns, and mobilize its own domestic resources for a program of development." It was clear that the United States had no intention of providing funds for a futile operation and would, on the contrary, insist upon effective steps by the recipient countries to complement U.S. financial aid with the self-help which only those nations could provide. "Even at the start," President Kennedy went on to say, "such measures will be a condition of assistance from the social fund. Priorities will depend not merely on need, but on the demonstrated readiness of each government to make the institutional improvements which promise lasting social progress."

Urgings from the United States for internal reforms in Latin American economic policies and practices are old stuff. They have had a less than satisfactory effect, and have often been met with charges of "intervention." What made it possible for President Kennedy to speak so directly of conditions that would govern the extension of assistance from the proposed social progress fund was the fact that a new formula had been found whereby those conditions could be accepted. It was no longer a case of the United States seeming to impose conditions on Latin American countries or of the latter implicitly threatening to turn to the Communist orbit if U.S. help were not forthcoming without strings attached. Both the United States and the Latin American countries have now joined in a common statement of a problem and its solution. The solution requires positive acts of faith on both sides: the assumption by Latin Americans of a responsibility to do something fundamental about their antiquated and inadequate social system; the assumption by the United States of a readiness to extend a new type of financial assistance with which to make social reform and economic development financially possible. The traditional tug-of-war between the borrower and the lender, the seller and the buyer, was to an important degree resolved in a common endeavor aiming at a goal accepted by both parties.

The pattern of increasing reliance on multilateral procedures adopted in the Bogotá program was further developed in the administration of the $500 million social progress fund appropriated by the U.S. Congress in 1961 for use in Latin America. The United States turned over $394 million of this fund to the Inter-American Development Bank for administration under a trust agreement. Thus, the U.S. government transferred to an international organization of twenty countries (Cuba is not a member of the Bank) the authority to disburse a fund provided solely by the United States for the direct benefit of the other member governments. The agreement makes clear, however, what the purpose of this trust fund is. Principally it is "to support the efforts of the Latin American countries that are prepared to initiate or expand effective institutional improvements and to adopt measures to employ efficiently their own resources with a view to achieving greater social progress and more balanced economic growth." The Bank, as administrator of the trust fund, is to give continuous consideration to the institutional improvements which a country is initiating or expanding, and to favor projects or programs that are related to effective self-help measures.

As one member of the Bank, the United States of course has a voice in the decisions taken. With regard to the approval of projects it may well have a technical veto. However, positive action requires the favorable decision of the Latin American members. The important thing is that the United States has, through this trust agreement, given further demonstration of its fundamental faith in the purpose and policies of the other members of the Inter-American System.

A multilateral procedure is also being followed with respect to review of the country plans that will form the basis for economic and social development loans under the Alliance for Progress. Each country will, of course, prepare its own national plan of development. However, responsibility for reviewing and assisting in the preparation of these plans has been given to the O.A.S. A key step in the planning process is provided by a panel of nine "high-level experts," who have been named by the O.A.S. to serve in an advisory capacity to the member governments. On the request of governments (and governments will usually find it advantageous to make the request) these experts, along with others brought in on an *ad hoc* basis, are available to analyze the country plans in the light of the objectives and policies set forth in the Act of Bogotá and the Charter of Punta del Este, and to report their findings not only to the respective governments but also to the international lending institutions from which funds will be sought to carry out the programs. For this and related purposes the United States has made available $6 million to the O.A.S. Progress in the preparation and execution of the various country programs will be reviewed annually by the IA-ECOSOC in fulfillment of its new function.

The United States has by no means placed entire responsibility for the Alliance for Progress upon the O.A.S. and related agencies. A major part of the responsibility remains in the hands of the agencies of the U.S. government—especially the Agency for International Development (AID) and the Export-Import Bank—working directly with the individual Latin American governments. Moreover, a large part of the foreign capital needed by the Latin American countries is expected to come from private sources, while additional amounts, both public and private, are being sought in other parts of the world, notably Europe and Japan.

Yet the significance of the role established for the international and especially inter-American agencies is not to be underestimated. The Alliance for Progress is by its very nature a cooperative, joint enterprise. It arose out of several years of discussion of the need for more active economic and social cooperation through the O.A.S., and against the background of the long evolution of principles of international cooperation through the inter-American system. The Alliance was developed at two O.A.S. meetings—Bogotá in 1960 and Punta del Este in 1961—and will be reviewed annually in the future at meetings of a rejuvenated organ of the O.A.S., the Inter-American Economic and Social Council. Under the general aegis of the Alliance, there are brought together three international agencies working in the inter-American scene (the O.A.S., the Inter-American Development Bank, and the U.N. Economic Commission for Latin America) whose top officers now form a coordinating committee to guide the activities of all three organizations in all aspects of the Alliance. There is no doubt that the combination of all these developments has given a new injection of political vigor to the Inter-American System that can have profound repercussions on its growth, strength, and capacity to serve the entire hemisphere community.

The new policies, procedures, and arrangements for the role of the inter-American agencies in the Alliance for Progress have been so recently established, and the functions involved are so broad, that it is impossible to forecast with any degree of certainty how they will work out. Time and events will show—perhaps more slowly than we would like—whether the concept of the Alliance for Progress and its new emphasis upon multilateral procedures will evoke from the Latin American countries a sufficient response to take the drastic steps needed for its success. In the economic and social field, as in the area of political progress, the future performance of the O.A.S. remains one of uncertainty colored with hope.

## 5. *Cuba and Communism*

Likewise uncertain is the prospect of effective action through the O.A.S. in the protection of the American nations from the subversive efforts of the Communist powers and their agents during the period of economic and social upheaval. The results of the Eighth Meeting of Consultation of Ministers of Foreign Affairs at Punta del Este, in January 1962, constituted a definite step forward from the severely restrained position taken by the foreign ministers at San José in 1960. The principal decisions taken at Punta del Este regarding the problem of Cuba and communism were two. The ministers first declared that the principles of communism were incompatible with the principles of the Inter-American System—a proposition on which all but Cuba agreed. They then, by the bare majority of two-thirds which the Rio Treaty requires, voted to exclude the present government of Cuba from participation in the Inter-American System, leaving it up to the various organs, especially the Council of the O.A.S., to take the necessary steps to that end.[8] It was on this vote that six countries—Argentina, Bolivia, Brazil, Chile, Ecuador and Mexico, comprising two-thirds of the population of Latin America—parted company with the United States by abstaining.

The disagreement at Punta del Este over the exclusion of the Castro government from Inter-American bodies did not reflect any substantial difference of opinion regarding communism as a doctrine or a political system—witness the vote in favor of the first proposition. The failure of the six countries to accompany the United States and the Caribbean group that was demanding tougher action against the Castro regime may be attributed to other factors. Some of these six governments no doubt felt that at that moment Cuba, even to the degree it was associated with the Communist bloc, was no serious

[8] In a separate resolution, also passed by 20-1 (Cuba opposed), the ministers voted to exclude the government of Cuba from the Inter-American Defense Board forthwith, this organ being a creation of the Meeting of Foreign Ministers and not governed by any treaty or convention.

threat to their independence or internal political equilibrium; whereas if they voted for and imposed sanctions, sympathy for Castro would increase and add to their domestic political problems. Another factor was a genuine doubt that the exclusion of the government of a member state from the O.A.S. was legally correct under the Charter, which contains no provision for such action. A feeling also existed in some circles that even though communism was incompatible with the principles of the Inter-American System, it was Cuba's right to adopt communism, and that only the Cuban people could decide upon a different course. Thus, in the minds of the six, nonintervention still weighed more heavily than any fear of aggression by Communist powers or by *Fidelismo*.

It is clear that considerably more progress must be made in the development of confidence on the part of the Latin American peoples in the declared purposes of the O.A.S. and in the policies of the United States before more vigorous action against the Communist menace now centered in Cuba can be adopted. Yet if the Alliance for Progress achieves success and the people of the Latin American countries perceive more clearly the value, to their interests and goals, of the principles surrounding the O.A.S., they will inevitably also support the measures necessary to protect this system from aggressive forces that aim at its disintegration and failure. The definite, if limited, progress made from Santiago to San José to Punta del Este supports this view.

# VI

# Facing the Future

The Inter-American System, despite the strain induced by the Cuban question, stands today on the threshold of a new era of vitality and growth. Under the decisions incorporated in the Act of Bogotá and the agreements of Punta del Este, its agencies have been given an important role in the task of promoting the far-reaching and profound transformation of the political, economic, and social scene that is demanded by the peoples of Latin America. In carrying out these new assignments, and in strengthening the political defense of the continent against Communist aggression, the regional organization also faces new and complex problems that will severely test its adequacy as an instrument of inter-American relations.

From the standpoint of the United States, and from that of Latin America as well, the failure of the O.A.S. to measure up to that challenge would be a disaster. This country has placed its confidence in the proposition that its vital interests in this hemisphere can and will be protected and pursued in collaboration with Latin America. If it ever has to fall back on unilateral action, taken without the consent or against the will of the Latin American peoples, it may gain momentary security at the price of lasting insecurity. The United States cannot, therefore, take the O.A.S. lightly or ignore what it stands for, even when it is a cause of frustration or acts as a brake on necessary action. On the other hand, the Latin American states must take account of the vital importance of the O.A.S. to them. If they attempt irresponsible use of their numerical strength in the O.A.S., if they carry to extremes the doctrine of nonintervention, if they leave the United States no alternative but to act unilaterally to protect itself, they will have destroyed not only the basis of hemispheric cooperation for progress but all hope of a secure future for themselves.

How well the O.A.S. will fulfill its expanded role is perhaps the key question in inter-American relations today. History gives no clear answer, for the past record of the Organization ranges from brilliant achievement to stultified inactivity. It has won great successes, and experienced dismal failures; it has moved ahead on waves of emotion, and bogged down in maladministration and slavish subordination to procedure and precedent. At times it has accepted challenges boldly, and at others timidly evaded issues of major importance. In its variegated career it has reflected policies that converged and policies that conflicted as well as the human nature of the peoples of its member countries both in their strengths and in their weaknesses.

In the period the O.A.S. is now entering, the successful performance of its new and larger role will call for action along three principal lines. First is the extension by the governments of a more vigorous support for the Organization and the improvement of their procedures for dealing with it. Second is the improvement and modernization of the Organization itself. Third, and most important, is the adoption by the United States and the Latin American nations, through the O.A.S., of policies that are realistically related to the problems of the day and that will adequately guide the agencies of the inter-American system in dealing with those problems.

### *1. Support by Governments*

The task of making the O.A.S. work starts within the governments of the member states. The first requirement is a conviction on their part that the multilateral procedure inherent in its use is a worthwhile and desirable way of meeting problems common to the American nations, including those which involve basic national interests. Such a conviction now appears to reside in virtually all the member governments of the O.A.S. It is implicit in the long tradition of their collective association and confirmed in the recent decisions of Bogotá and Punta del Este. But this positive attitude must be implemented by a number of practical measures to assure to the Organization the necessary technical, material, and human resources and moral support to enable it to do its job. Much remains to be done.

The member states have traditionally displayed an all too liberal predilection for endowing the O.A.S. with grandiose functions and creating paper solutions to fundamental problems. But the Organization can no longer afford the luxury of resting upon the rhetorical and oratorical expressions that characterized inter-American deliberations for so many decades. It is faced today with a host of intricate and complex problems of a technical, political, and administrative nature which cannot be resolved by improvised flights of imagination. These problems require the application of increasingly specialized knowledge, and the undertaking of often dull and boring work that has relatively little appeal in comparison to the heady wine of oratory under the spotlight of international conferences.

In concrete terms, this means that the member states must improve their home organizations, primarily in the foreign offices, that deal with O.A.S. activities, as well as their representation in the numerous agencies of the regional system. Adequate attention to these matters, moreover, calls for better contact and communication between representatives on such bodies as the Council and their respective governments in order that the latter may understand more thoroughly the nature of the problems which their representatives are considering and give them adequate guidance. Governments must also be prepared to face the unpleasant necessity of footing the bill for the costs of expanded O.A.S. activities.

There are, of course, limits on the rate at which the Organization can be expanded and given new tasks. The failure of member states to do all that is called for in support of the O.A.S. is not by any means due simply to a lack of will. Severe inadequacies in the resources of many of the Latin American countries impose barriers to greater contributions on their part in men and in money. Technical personnel is still in very short supply in most of the other American republics, making it difficult for governments to assign adequately trained people to the manifold tasks which membership in the O.A.S. (as well as in other international organizations) imposes upon them. The availability of financial resources is likewise a limiting factor, even though the sums involved hardly seem burdensome. For the fiscal year ending June 30, 1961, the regular budgets of the O.A.S. and its constituent agencies totaled in the neighborhood of $15 million.[1] Under the negotiated quota system adopted some years ago, the United States contributes about two-thirds of this amount, the twenty Latin American countries, one-third. Even assuming a willingness on the part of the United States to increase its annual contribution to more than the present $10 million per year in order to support a greater effort, the possibility of doing so is limited by the capacity and willingness of the Latin American countries to approve higher budgets and assume correspondingly higher assessments.

In several instances the United States has made special contributions and grants to O.A.S. agencies above and beyond its regular quota, so that activities essential to particular inter-American programs could go on. The allocation by the United States of $6 million from the Alliance for Progress to the O.A.S. for assistance in economic and social planning and related purposes is a case in point. However desirable such a procedure may be from the standpoint of making possible the execution of important activities, there are limits to its application. The essence of the O.A.S. is a sharing of responsibility, and if this character is to be preserved it is essential to avoid having virtually the full burden of supporting cooperative activities carried by only one member of the association. There is a

---

[1] This figure does not, of course, include the Inter-American Development Bank, which has its separate organization and system of financing.

point beyond which the entire program would cease to be cooperative and would become instead a unilateral activity cloaked in the mere semblance of multilateral responsibility.

The vastly increased significance of the O.A.S. in the international relations of the United States at this time, and the influence which this country must inevitably exercise in it, make it essential that the U.S. government also review its own policies and procedures with respect to the Organization and its own representation in O.A.S. bodies. For many years the O.A.S. received only routine, and sometimes grudging, attention on the part of the top officials of this government, who confined themselves to essentially *pro forma* participation in its activities and occasional attendance at major conferences. One of the most constructive features of recent relations with the O.A.S. has been the increased active, personal attention of the President and officers of cabinet rank to the substantive problems under consideration there. Their continued active participation in the affairs of the O.A.S. is essential to its effectiveness in coming years. The Meetings of Consultation of Ministers of Foreign Affairs and the meetings on the ministerial level of the IA-ECOSOC will be increasingly important in determining the policy and action of the Organization as it moves forward in the Alliance for Progress. To assist these high officials, a larger corps of technical officers, thoroughly experienced in the complexities of the O.A.S. and its activities, is also needed.

The Congress has never adopted any specific legislation to govern the participation of the United States in the O.A.S. So gradually did the Inter-American System grow, and so unreservedly has its existence and the major role of the United States in it been endorsed by this country, that our participation has rested largely on informal understanding and accepted practice. For years the U.S. Congress appropriated funds for the support of the Pan American Union on the basis of a convention signed in 1928 which had been ratified by the United States but never went into force because of the failure of some of the Latin American governments to complete their ratifications. Not until the Charter of the O.A.S. took legal effect in 1949 did a firm treaty basis for the Organization come into being. Even then, the U.S. Congress enacted no implementing legislation, as it had in the case of the United Nations.

Legislation, if not absolutely necessary, would be appropriate in order to establish the arrangements for the representation of this government in the main bodies of the O.A.S. While representation in the meetings on the ministerial level may appropriately be exercised ex officio by the secretary of state or of the treasury, the position of representative on the Council of the Organization deserves special attention as one of increasing responsibility. At times this official by his vote commits the United States to action under the Treaty of Rio de Janeiro, including the imposition of sanctions on an aggressor state. It would be proper for this position and the authority of its incumbent to be established by legislation, and for the appointment of the representative to require confirmation by the Senate.

Of greater importance from the legislative standpoint is the question of the authority of the president to commit the United States in a vote on sanctions under the Treaty of Rio de Janeiro. It will be recalled that sanctions were applied for the first time in the history of the treaty in the case of the Dominican Republic at the Sixth Meeting of Foreign Ministers in 1960. Fortunately, the resolution that was adopted presented no grave legal problem for the United States. But had the issue of the complete severance of economic relations, or the use of military force, been pressed by a two-thirds majority of the member states, the position of the United States would have been most embarrassing. For at present it is at least open to serious doubt whether the executive branch of the government can agree to complete severance of economic relations with another country, or to the use of U.S. military force as part of an O.A.S. collective action, without authorization of the Congress. At best, it would be necessary in such an event to resort to existing legislation adopted primarily with reference to other situations—the Trading with the Enemy Act for example—but there is no assurance it would be adequate to cover the action desired.

Some of these questions were encountered when the case of Guatemala was brought up before the O.A.S. in 1954; they were not resolved at that time because the immediate need for action disappeared with the overthrow of the Arbenz regime. Although the sanctions imposed upon the Dominican Republic in 1960 and those voted against the Castro regime in January 1962, stirred no legal controversy—Cuba especially presented no problem in view of Castro's ties with the Communist bloc—the uncertainty and the need for clarifying legislation remained.

## 2. *Organizational Improvements*

Stronger support by the member governments, then, is the first requisite for a stronger O.A.S. A more effective organization of the regional agency itself is the second.

The efficiency of the O.A.S. has suffered from the effects of its haphazard growth and the tendency of its member governments to set up new agencies instead of making those already in existence work. When the Charter was drafted at Bogotá, an effort was made to consolidate the structure of the Organization. Some existing committees, commissions, and agencies were in fact eliminated or merged with the reorganized Pan American Union. However, even under the Charter of Bogotá a superfluity of agencies has persisted, and some of the bad habits of the past have continued to exercise their baleful influence on the Organization.

One bad habit that has plagued the O.A.S. over the years is the seemingly irresistible tendency of meetings and conferences to adopt resolutions calling for broad programs that are completely beyond the scope and ability of existing agencies to carry out. The very processing of these resolutions is a time-consuming operation. Their substantive review by the Council and the secretariat, and the arrangement of a decent interment for the great majority that cannot possibly be implemented, occupy a vast amount of time, labor, and funds which should be devoted to more useful activities. Mention has already been made of how the assignment of unrealistic functions

to the Inter-American Economic and Social Council under the old
statute was in part responsible for its failure to make a moderately
constructive contribution to inter-American economic relations, and
how this led to the creation of new committees and agencies outside of the framework of the Charter, thus further complicating the
organizational confusion. The tendency of O.A.S. bodies in any
event to dedicate inordinate amounts of time and energy to procedural problems has been accentuated by this process. A strong
secretariat might conceivably be able to check this tendency and
guide the various councils and committees into more constructive
paths. However, the O.A.S. secretariat, itself hampered by the
growing pains of rapid expansion and a lack of experienced personnel, is hardly in a position to exercise such leadership. In the O.A.S.
the secretariat has traditionally been more definitely subordinated
to the representative bodies and more restricted in its initiative than
is the case in the United Nations.[2]

Not only the secretariat, but other principal organs require
strengthening and modernization if the O.A.S. is to perform its
indicated role in coming years. One need only look at the example
given by the Inter-American Conference, according to the Charter
"the supreme organ" of the O.A.S. It "decides the general action
and policy of the Organization" and "has the authority to consider
any matter relating to friendly relations among the American States."
The Charter, drawing upon a custom established in the early years
of the Inter-American System, stipulates that "the Conference shall
convene every five years." It thus perpetuated a system of inter-
American meetings modeled after the First Pan American Conference held in Washington. This conference lasted from October 2,
1889, to April 19, 1890, a large part of the time of the delegates
being occupied by a railroad trip around the United States as
guests of the U.S. government. The leisurely and diverting nature of
the conference was perhaps well suited to the tempo of travel and of

[2] For an informed comment, by a recognized authority, on the limitations
imposed upon the Secretary-General by the Council, see William Manger, *Pan
America in Crisis* (Washington: Public Affairs Press, 1961), p. 79.

international affairs at that time. Unfortunately, the pattern thus established has been inadequately adjusted to contemporary requirements. As a result, the O.A.S. has as its highest authority an antiquated body that is virtually incapable of exercising its important functions. The fact that most conferences last at least one month virtually rules out the possibility that the secretary of state of the United States or foreign ministers of leading Latin American countries can attend for anything but a small part of its deliberations.

The situation of the Inter-American Conference is highlighted by the fact that at the present critical period of the O.A.S., when new ideas are being born and the need for decisions regarding "the general action and policy of the Organization" is greater than ever, it has not been possible to convoke the Eleventh Inter-American Conference that was originally scheduled to be held in 1959. For this unfortunate lapse, the established procedure, according to which the year and place are fixed five years in advance, is partly to blame. The projected date bore no relationship to the timing of urgent matters before the O.A.S. Such subjects as the problem of Cuba or the establishment of an Inter-American Development Bank had, therefore, to be considered at Meetings of Foreign Ministers, or other special conferences, which could be more easily arranged. The specific site, selected in 1954 for the conference to be held five years later, was Quito, Ecuador. But when the time approached, it became clear that both national and international political reasons made it virtually impossible to hold a conference in that city at the appointed time. Moreover, the elaborate and time-consuming procedure required to develop the agenda of the conference further obstructed the inclusion in the program of the really urgent matters facing the inter-American community. With the subjects of first importance thus excluded, the agenda was left with a list of subjects that were either too controversial, too complex, or too unimportant to deal with at any other time. Thus any substantive interest which the American governments might have had in holding the conference further declined, and it was repeatedly and inevitably postponed.

Whether or not the Eleventh Inter-American Conference is ever held, it is time that this antiquated system of conducting the affairs of a highly important international organization be corrected. This suggestion may well shock those who are deeply committed to the concept of the "supreme organ." However, the problem can easily be resolved without violating the constitutional precepts of the Charter. The solution is for the functions of the Inter-American Conference to be curtailed to those truly involving decisions concerning "the general action and policy of the Organization," and to have the Conference itself merged in all but name with the Meetings of Foreign Ministers. This would also require the delegation to other subsidiary bodies of much of the responsibility for the more routine and technical actions of the O.A.S., so that the foreign ministers could concentrate their attention upon issues of major importance, or attend to those matters, of which there are always some, which for constitutional reasons require the formal approval of the "supreme organ." Taking advantage of Article 36 of the Charter, which authorizes the holding of special conferences, the Inter-American Conference could become a title assumed by a Meeting of Foreign Ministers whenever it was necessary, and could then be scheduled with proper relationship to the sequence of international events.

The need for delegating downward the responsibility for many matters presently considered by high organs of the O.A.S. will be abundantly clear from a review of the subjects that have occupied the attention of the past sessions of the Inter-American Conference, and of the resolutions, recommendations, and other agreements adopted. They fall roughly into five main categories: major political pronouncements on matters of current concern, such as the resolution on communism of the Tenth (Caracas) Conference; major treaties, such as the Charter of the O.A.S. adopted at the Ninth (Bogotá) Conference; resolutions creating new agencies of the O.A.S., or revising the competence or character of existing ones; resolutions and recommendations dealing with numerous routine juridical, economic, social, and cultural subjects usually of a semi-technical nature; and, finally, decisions passing on to another agency of the

O.A.S.—or even to the next Conference—the study of subjects on which for one reason or another it proved impossible to take action.

Few of the multitude of resolutions and recommendations that have occupied its sessions actually require or merit the attention of the Inter-American Conference. Major treaties do; but they should always be drafted by the Council and submitted to the Conference in virtually final text for formal approval. If a treaty involves issues of such importance as to require detailed consideration and negotiation by high officials, a special session of the Conference should be called, as was done in 1947 to draft the Treaty of Rio de Janeiro, for which excellent preparatory work had already been done. The vast majority of resolutions and recommendations on problems of an essentially routine or technical character should preferably be avoided entirely; often they merely serve to confuse rather than help the efforts at which they are directed. To the extent that they are necessary—and this applies to only a minority of the vast assortment now resting quietly in the files of the O.A.S.—they should be the concern of a more appropriate organ. This might be the Council, or one of the excellent specialized, technical agencies and technical conferences that are already accomplishing most of the useful work in these fields.

A major improvement recently effected in the Meetings of Foreign Ministers has saved that organ from a fate similar to that of the Conference. Originally conceived as a personal consultation among the top foreign policy officials of the member countries, these meetings had acquired an increasingly elaborate character until they had developed into full-dress conferences, complete with protocol, committees and subcommittees, and numerous technical advisers. An informal meeting of foreign ministers held in Washington on the invitation of Secretary Dulles for two days in September 1958, again demonstrated the value of informal consultations. Following this unofficial precedent the Fifth, Sixth, Seventh, and Eighth Meetings of Consultation resumed their original character: agendas were limited to subjects requiring urgent attention, and the negotiations were carried on directly among the foreign ministers. This character of the meetings should be preserved so that they can continue to be held frequently—say once a year—without constituting an impossible drain on the time of their participants.

The downward delegation of authority should also place new and larger responsibilities on the Council of the O.A.S. This step is already forecast in the frequent referral to the Council of subjects which the Inter-American Conference or Meetings of Foreign Ministers do not have adequate opportunity to consider. The main criticism that can be made of the Council during recent years is for its tendency to dedicate itself to relatively unimportant procedural and technical issues, and to evade its responsibility for dealing with those of major importance. This is in part due to a lack of communication, in both a physical and intellectual sense, between some representatives on the Council and their governments. Foreign ministries in some cases have little understanding of what goes on in the Council; their representatives, finding it difficult to obtain adequate policy guidance, are thereby led to avoid decisions on major questions and to dedicate their efforts, if they feel so inclined, to the minor issues which predominate in the debates.

These comments by no means apply to all member governments; more and more of them are developing adequate systems of guidance for their representatives on Council matters. Two factors will accelerate this desirable development. As the Council receives responsibility for considering important policy matters, the governments will be forced to follow its problems with greater attention. And as the Meetings of Foreign Ministers take place more frequently and assign new tasks to the Council, the foreign offices will gain a more intimate understanding of what the Council is doing and what sort of instructions their representatives require. This was clearly evidenced, for example, in the execution by the Council of the tasks assigned to it by the Sixth Meeting of Foreign Ministers with respect to the sanctions imposed upon the Dominican Republic.

The most important function of the Council today is that of acting provisionally as Organ of Consultation under the Treaty of Rio de

Janeiro. This relationship between the Council and the Meeting of Foreign Ministers gives a clue to the further development of the Council's usefulness. If we visualize more frequent Meetings of Foreign Ministers, we can foresee a greatly expanded activity of the Council in preparing these meetings and in carrying out the decisions reached there. The Council should, in fact, become a sort of junior consultative body at which provisional agreements could be reached on a variety of issues, leaving only the central unresolved policy problems to the decision of the foreign ministers. Nothing in the Charter stands in the way of such a development.

The timid attitude of the member governments toward the assumption of authority by the Council is highlighted by the procedure developed under the Treaty of Rio. At the time of the Nicaraguan and Panamanian cases in 1959 it was widely observed that the juridical formula of convoking a Meeting of Consultation of Ministers of Foreign Affairs without any thought of its ever taking place, solely to permit the Council of the O.A.S. to act in its stead, had resulted in a depreciation of the collective security system of the treaty. It is, of course, unrealistic to expect the foreign ministers of the twenty-one American republics to drop their other responsibilities for national and international affairs and rush to a meeting just because a boatload of one hundred bearded warriors has landed on the coast of a Caribbean country. Yet it is demeaning to the whole concept of hemisphere consultation to continue to send out false alarms for Meetings of Foreign Ministers that are never expected to be held. It is entirely proper that some representative organ, on a lower rank than that of foreign ministers, be authorized to deal with such situations. The Rio Treaty was never intended to be applied to such minor disturbances as those characterized by the cases of Panama and Nicaragua; it was to deal with major problems of aggression and threats to the sovereignty and independence of states—problems that would in truth command the personal attention of the foreign ministers. The Council was granted authority to act provisionally only to permit rapid collective action in urgent situations pending the actual gathering of the foreign ministers.

The fear of giving power directly to the Council, however, has prevented a more logical and rational solution to the problem. This fear accounts for the fact that the Council does not consider itself authorized even to investigate a situation that is called to its attention until it has issued the convocation for the Meeting of Consultation. It would seem logical that if the Council has the duty, under the Rio Treaty and the Charter of the O.A.S., of deciding whether to convoke the Meeting of Consultation of Ministers of Foreign Affairs, it should have the power to assemble sufficient information to enable it to make that decision wisely. This would imply that in a doubtful case the Council, before deciding to convoke the Meeting of Consultation, would establish a committee to assemble information, travel to the scene of trouble if necessary, and render a report to the Council on whether the facts warranted throwing the full machinery of the Treaty of Rio into action. However, the opposite view has prevailed in the Council, due to the strict construction placed upon the Charter and to the fear of some members of the Council that, once a committee were set up and sent into the field, it would exceed the limited function of fact-finding given to it and become actively involved in the controversy.

Perhaps the performances of some of the "investigating committees" sent out under the Treaty of Rio in past years give some grounds for these fears: the committees have never been accused of a lack of enterprise or enthusiasm. Yet it is folly to prejudice the rational development of the O.A.S. collective security system because of the performance of one or two committees during the early experiences with the Rio Treaty. Furthermore, it would seem reasonable to expect that a committee sent out by the Council to investigate a situation as a preliminary step to determining whether the treaty should be invoked would act with far greater caution than one sent out as representing the Council when already acting provisionally as Organ of Consultation.

The O.A.S. peace machinery would also be substantially improved by strengthening the Inter-American Peace Committee. It should be empowered to take cognizance of any dispute between American states when the use of forceful sanctions under the Treaty of Rio de Janeiro is not contemplated. The Council, on receiving a request for a Meeting of Foreign Ministers, should be empowered to refer such a dispute to the Peace Committee if its investigation of the situation led the Council to conclude that a Meeting of Foreign Ministers was not required. The Peace Committee should also have restored to it the authority, of which it was deprived in 1956, to take up any case brought before it by an American state without having to obtain the prior consent of other parties to the controversy. These measures would fill the need for an O.A.S. organ competent to consider the many lesser controversies that arise in inter-American relations and yet do not justify the application of the elaborate and powerful machinery of the Treaty of Rio de Janeiro.

The suggested changes would do much to equip the O.A.S. for the more substantial part in inter-American affairs which coming decades may be expected to demand of it. They would not, let it be admitted, produce a perfectly streamlined organization. There would still remain a number of dangling committees and councils, some of which contribute little to effective action in a way commensurate with their cost, and others of which have relapsed into a completely moribund state. These structural problems, along with those of strangling procedures and bureaucratic inefficiencies, must be faced as part of the business of the orderly maintenance and improvement of the Organization.

Of particular significance for the future are the problems associated with the new and enlarged responsibilities of the O.A.S. in the economic and social field. Three important forward strides recently taken have already been referred to: the reorganization of the Inter-American Economic and Social Council, the establishment of the Inter-American Development Bank, and the strengthening of the staff of the Pan American Union. There remains the problem of working out the long-range relationship between the Bank, the Pan American Union as secretariat of the O.A.S., and the United Nations Economic Commission for Latin America and other U.N. agencies. At present this relationship is somewhat vague, and it is probably well that it remain flexible until time and experience have further clarified what the precise role of each agency should be in the continuing program of inter-American economic cooperation.

### *3. The Bedrock of Policy*

A reconsideration of certain basic policies is another requisite for the successful functioning of the O.A.S. in the coming decades, for organization alone provides no more than a means to an end. Any suggestion that the principles and policies which have been formulated and refined by the devoted labor of jurists and statesmen over more than a century of debate should be tampered with at all will shock many devotees of the Inter-American System. Let it therefore be said at the start that there is no thought here of jettisoning the basic principles on which the O.A.S. is founded. The juridical equality of sovereign states, nonintervention, solidarity in defense of the independence of the Americas, and cooperation for the achievement of common goals continue to be sound and respected principles. But they must at any stage of history be related to the circumstances of the time; otherwise they become formalistic shibboleths that may even stand in the way of the achievement of the true purposes they were meant to serve. Thus the policies by which these principles are implemented must from time to time be reviewed, clarified, and restated to retain their touch with reality.

The keystone in the arch of inter-American doctrine is the principle of nonintervention. Inevitably, therefore, it has repeatedly been the key point of policy discussion. The present time is no exception, for if the principle of nonintervention has served to hold together the structure of Pan Americanism, it also threatens to become a major obstacle to the further development of inter-American cooperation and to the achievement of the very purposes for which the Inter-American System was designed.

The principle of nonintervention—or more properly the doctrine associated with the term—has its peculiar character in the Inter-American System over and above its place in general international law. In this hemisphere it arose out of the internal weaknesses of the Latin American countries during the nineteenth century, when political and economic turmoil and instability in various countries invited the intervention of stronger powers wishing to protect the interests, and often the lives, of their citizens. The doctrine, after the original period of the struggle for independence from European colonial powers, came to be directed principally at the United States, the closest and most active world power, which not only threatened but actually practiced intervention with force in several Latin American countries. There was, accordingly, an important and realistic basis for the development of the nonintervention principle. The process whereby the Latin American states formulated this doctrine and forced the United States to accept it as a condition of Pan American cooperation has been described earlier.

It is important to recall not only what the nonintervention principle was intended to do in protecting weaker states from violations of their sovereignty, political independence, and territorial integrity, but also what it was not intended to do. It was not intended to isolate each state from every other one, so that absolute sovereignty and nationalism could reign unchecked by the larger interests of the inter-American community. It was not intended to provide international protection for arbitrary tyrants, so that they could with impunity violate the most fundamental human rights and outrage the conscience of mankind. Nor was it intended to facilitate indirect aggression by a state or political force against the political institutions of another state and its people. Yet these universally deplored developments have in fact been encouraged at various times by the nonintervention doctrine as applied in its extreme form.

In their zeal to establish a doctrine that would put Uncle Sam in the tightest possible juridical strait jacket, Latin American jurists and political leaders carried the nonintervention doctrine to unrealistic extremes. The language of Article 15 of the Charter of the O.A.S. is so broad that it lends itself to virtually any interpretation which a state that feels itself aggrieved wishes to place upon The principle, first directed at intervention by force, was exten to cover all kinds of acts that might be viewed as pressure. It has even been used to condemn inaction: e.g., failure of the United States to take action against a dictator has been condemned as intervention on his behalf. It was as though the proponents of this doctrine wished not so much to confine the use of U.S. power to acceptable legal channels as to exorcise it completely.

The most serious aspect of the extreme development of the doctrine is its application not only to unilateral acts of a state but to actions of the O.A.S. as well. "No State *or group of States* has the right to intervene," says Article 15 of the Charter. While the words "or group of States" do not necessarily apply to the Organization of American States which, as a juridical entity, is more than a mere "group of States," the article has widely been interpreted as enjoining the O.A.S. from any action that might fall under the broad and absolute rule of nonintervention. This has been so despite the obvious intent of the Charter to exempt action by the Organization for the maintenance of peace and security from the nonintervention rule, as is clearly stated in Article 19.

The most flagrant recent example of the miscarriage of the nonintervention principle is the case of Cuba. Here the principle has, by its powerful inhibitive force, prevented effective action by the inter-American community to defend the hemisphere from the extension of Soviet-bloc influence and political control. It has had the effect of protecting an intervention from outside the continent and has made a mockery of the right of self-determination.

A more general problem raised by the nonintervention doctrine today is that it stands in the way of action by the O.A.S. that is essential to the achievement of economic, social, and political goals that the peoples of Latin America most earnestly seek. The objec-
Act of Bogotá and the Alliance for Progress call for
in the internal institutions, laws, and governmental
participating states. These changes have been
and necessary by the Latin American mem-
by the United States. The United States has,
that its financial support of the Alliance for

Progress is conditioned upon the carrying out of these basic social and economic changes within a framework of political freedom. Thus the O.A.S. and its related agencies have become in effect the guarantors of the basic agreement underlying the Alliance for Progress, which involves the extension of financial aid by the United States on the one hand and the undertaking of reforms by the Latin American countries on the other.

So deeply do these required reforms penetrate into the internal life and institutions of each Latin American country, and so directly do they impinge upon long-established privileges and vested interests, that opposition to their enactment will be certain. Most large landowners are not likely to display all of a sudden the social responsibility that they have failed to demonstrate for hundreds of years, and to accept meekly the shearing of their power, prestige, and possessions. Large businesses and wealthy individuals long used to skillful tax evasion as a matter of course are not to be expected to accept a larger and more effective tax bite without fighting back. Labor groups have already shown their readiness to use political power to oppose the belt-tightening features of anti-inflation programs. The list of issues and interested parties could be expanded at length.

Opposition to these changes will not, of course, take the form of open antagonism to the changes themselves. It will be indirect, drawing upon issues and principles that otherwise enjoy popular support. Practically no issue can engender so great an emotional response in Latin America as that of intervention. It is virtually inevitable that the opposition to social reforms in many countries will seize upon this issue, charging the United States or the O.A.S., or both, with intervention in internal affairs if the demands for specific reforms are pressed and financial aid withheld until such changes are effected. Latin American supporters of reforms maintain that conditions placed upon the extension of economic aid are not to be confused with intervention. However, the extreme form to which the non-intervention doctrine has been carried, extending not only to unilateral measures but to action by a group of states, gives strong grounds for believing that no opportunity to drag in the principle will be overlooked when the issue is joined.

If this is true in economic and social affairs, it will be even more true in the political field, the most sensitive area of Latin America's concern over intervention. As compared with the economic field, relatively little careful thought has been given in recent years to the problem of political development in Latin America and the role of the O.A.S. with respect to it. This fact is highlighted by a comparison of two agencies established in the last few years: the Inter-American Development Bank on the one hand and the Inter-American Commission on Human Rights on the other. The Bank was established as a result of a long and expert negotiation, in the course of which all major issues were faced, debated, and finally resolved to the satisfaction of all. Its procedures and functions have been developed since that time with skill and care. The Human Rights Commission, on the other hand, was set up as a hasty improvisation and with no well-thought-out role or procedure. Since its establishment it has floundered about in varied attempts to find a useful function and field of action for itself. It has proved unable to break the crust of the entrenched thinking on intervention.

It is clear that progress toward the economic, social, and political goals which the American republics have set for themselves in the framework of the Inter-American System calls for the exercise of great skill and restraint, along with insistent pressure. Special demands are placed upon the United States in this regard because of the predominant role this country must inevitably play in every aspect of the multilateral endeavor. Yet even the best efforts will be of limited value if the inhibitions associated with the nonintervention principle are not somewhat relaxed.

Among the specific requirements in this connection are a clearer and more realistic understanding of what intervention means, and what it does not mean, so far as the application of the nonintervention principle is concerned. Attempts to write a comprehensive legal definition of intervention are futile. However, the intervention which the doctrine outlaws should be understood to consist of arbitrary acts of any government to impose its will on another by the use of force or other coercive measures that violate the sovereignty of the other state. The emphasis should be on the *arbitrary* and *coercive* character of the measures, which are taken by *unilateral* decision. The concept of intervention should certainly not apply to action taken by the O.A.S. pursuant to established procedures. This view is explicitly stated in the Charter, which exempts from the nonintervention rule "measures taken for the maintenance of peace and security in accordance with existing treaties." These measures should be understood to include not only those taken against a military aggressor, but any measures which the O.A.S. adopts, in accordance with established treaty procedures, in order to meet attempts at subversion or any threat or act of aggression against one or more American states. It should also be clearly established that the term intervention could not be applied to efforts taken in accordance with agreed-upon procedures, through the O.A.S., to carry out an agreement such as the Act of Bogotá or Charter of Punta del Este.

Consideration should be given to the conclusion of a treaty to cover the expanding role of the O.A.S. in the political sphere. Heretofore the United States has refused to consider any treaty dealing with the observance of human rights or political democracy on the grounds that such a document would invade the powers reserved to the individual states under our federal constitution. This opposition has been due in part to the nature of the treaties suggested by the other American governments. While sufficient work has not yet been done on this subject to formulate any precise ideas, it should be possible to envisage a treaty covering certain basic policies, for example: (a) a more definite statement than that now contained in the O.A.S. Charter of the adherence of the American states to the principles of representative democracy and respect for human rights; (b) a recognition of the common interest in the development of democratic political institutions and the right of any state to express itself freely on that subject without being charged with intervention; and (c) a willingness of member states to cooperate with a reconstituted Inter-American Commission on Human Rights that would be authorized to study the observance of human rights in all member countries and consult with the government regarding legal, educational, or other measures that would be helpful in promoting a greater understanding of and respect for human rights. Such a treaty would confirm the principles to which the O.A.S. adheres, but would not attempt to set up an international system to review and pass upon the judicial processes of individual governments—a step for which the American republics are still not prepared.

The measures suggested above would substantially strengthen and clarify the framework of principle within which the Inter-American System operates. The more intimate the collaboration among the American states becomes, and the more deeply they are committed to the pursuit of practical economic and social objectives, the more necessary it is to reach agreement on the fundamental premises within which such cooperation takes place. A democratic society, whether of persons or states, can only flourish if its members accept certain basic principles of conduct and guide themselves accordingly. If such responsibility is not voluntarily assumed, the society will either disintegrate or fall under the sway of an authoritarian power which will impose the necessary rules.

This brings us to the problem of the delinquent state. What should be done with regard to a member state of the O.A.S. that violates important principles of the Organization and obstructs the efforts of its members to achieve their agreed objectives? This problem becomes most serious with regard to indirect aggression, an act which usually involves some form of violation of the nonintervention principle. What if the government of an American state, voluntarily or otherwise, comes under the control of an extracontinental power without any overt use of military force?

The key to this problem of the delinquent state lies in the logical proposition that no state can expect to enjoy the advantages and protection of the O.A.S. if it persists in a willful violation of the principles of the Organization. In specific terms, no state should be permitted to hide behind the principle of nonintervention while violating that very principle itself or otherwise undermining inter-

American solidarity and cooperation. This point was made by Eduardo Rodríguez Larreta in his proposal of 1945. The main trouble with the Uruguayan Foreign Minister's initiative was that the only solution offered was "collective intervention," and on that rock his proposal foundered. But the basic idea that some collective sanction should be imposed upon a delinquent member of the Western Hemisphere family is as old as the idea of continental confederation.

The drafters of the Panama Treaty of 1826 saw the problem clearly. They provided for the expulsion from the projected federation of any state that committed aggression on a member state in violation of the treaty pledges or failed to heed the decisions of the Assembly when it had previously agreed to accept such decisions; and for the expulsion of any state that changed its (republican) form of government. Again in 1848, the projected Treaty of Lima provided that the members would "suspend all of their obligations" in regard to a member state that opened hostilities against another member or that refused to comply with the decisions of the Congress, "in order that the disobedient Republic should feel the consequences of its infidelity."[3] It would seem that the O.A.S., which is now rapidly becoming an ever more vital instrument for the achievement of the common purposes of the American republics, should do no less than adopt the rule that the members would "suspend all of their obligations" (including the protection afforded by the Treaty of Rio de Janeiro, the nonintervention rule, and the Convention on the Rights and Duties of States in the Event of Civil Strife) toward an American state that persistently and recalcitrantly violates basic principles which all member states are pledged to observe.

The strengthening of the policies and principles of the O.A.S. along those lines will require more than legal formulas and logical arguments. It will demand a substantial increase in public confidence in the Organization and its purposes. The creation of this

[3] The texts of both the Panama and Lima treaties may be found in Robert N. Burr and Roland D. Hussey, eds., *Documents on Inter-American Cooperation* (Philadelphia: University of Pennsylvania Press, 1955).

greater confidence must begin with the United States, for it has in large measure been a fear of the United States, or at best an uncertainty as to its ultimate purposes, that has restrained the Latin American countries in granting authority to the Organization established at Rio de Janeiro and Bogotá. The historic change in U.S. policy expressed in the Act of Bogotá of 1960 and the Alliance for Progress should serve to reassure the Latin American peoples and create a basis for building a renewed confidence. A clarification of the nature of this change and a consistent and effective pursuit of the new course is now needed.

This means for the United States a deeper commitment of power and resources to the Inter-American System and the O.A.S. The issue before this country is not the simple one of choosing whether to rely exclusively upon a unilateral or upon a collective approach to hemisphere relations. It is a matter of achieving a balance between the wise and constructive exercise of the power and resources of the United States, which will for an indefinite future continue to predominate in the hemisphere, and the gradual but steady sharing of responsibility with the other American states through the Inter-American System, as the O.A.S. becomes capable of assuming such responsibility.

In so doing the United States will give evidence of its own confidence that there exists today, as there has existed in other critical periods of history, a fundamental coincidence of interests among the countries of the Western Hemisphere and therefore a sound and broadening base for international cooperation to assure their peace and security and their economic, social, and political progress. By building on this base we may, in partnership with the other American states, make a significant contribution to the development of new patterns of international cooperation. We may create through the Inter-American System some of the new political entities which in this stage of history are so needed for tasks that are clearly beyond the capacity of national states to accomplish.

If the outlook for the coming decade in inter-American affairs calls for greater and more positive efforts on the part of the United

States, it also presents an unprecedented challenge to Latin America. The good neighbors have an equal part in making the principles of the Inter-American System work. In the decade of the 1960s, the O.A.S. is called upon to carry out a far greater assignment than heretofore: that of helping to unite the efforts and the human and material resources of the hemisphere so that Latin America may restructure its economic and social system and so achieve material progress without sacrificing its liberties. It is now for the Latin American countries to accept the responsibility that is offered, to translate their repeated words into deeds, to take the initiative in effecting the needed changes they have so often demanded in their institutions, and to remove obstacles which obstruct progress toward their own clearly stated goals. Whether in the name of the Inter-American System, of the Alliance for Progress, or of the O.A.S. itself, there now lies the opportunity for Latin Americans to give new substance and meaning to the American idea which their own revered Bolívar so eloquently enunciated to the peoples of the new world as the basis for their unity, liberty, and progress.

# Index

*Publications of the*

# COUNCIL ON FOREIGN RELATIONS

FOREIGN AFFAIRS (quarterly), edited by Hamilton Fish Armstrong.

THE UNITED STATES IN WORLD AFFAIRS (annual). Volumes for 1931, 1932 and 1933, by Walter Lippmann and William O. Scroggs; for 1934-1935, 1936, 1937, 1938, 1939 and 1940, by Whitney H. Shepardson and William O. Scroggs; for 1945-1947, 1947-1948 and 1948-1949, by John C. Campbell; for 1949, 1950, 1951, 1952, 1953 and 1954, by Richard P. Stebbins; for 1955, by Hollis W. Barber; for 1956, 1957, 1958, 1959, 1960 and 1961 by Richard P. Stebbins.

DOCUMENTS ON AMERICAN FOREIGN RELATIONS (annual). Volume for 1952 edited by Clarence W. Baier and Richard P. Stebbins; for 1953 and 1954, edited by Peter V. Curl; for 1955, 1956, 1957, 1958 and 1959, edited by Paul E. Zinner; for 1960 and 1961, edited by Richard P. Stebbins.

POLITICAL HANDBOOK OF THE WORLD (annual), edited by Walter H. Mallory.

THE UNITED NATIONS: Structure for Peace, by Ernest A. Gross.

THE LONG POLAR WATCH: Canada and the Defense of North America, by Melvin Conant.

LATIN AMERICA: Diplomacy and Reality, by Adolf A. Berle.

ARMS AND POLITICS IN LATIN AMERICA (Revised Edition), by Edwin Lieuwen.

THE FUTURE OF UNDERDEVELOPED COUNTRIES: Political Implications of Economic Development (Revised Edition), by Eugene Staley.

SPAIN AND DEFENSE OF THE WEST: Ally and Liability, by Arthur P. Whitaker.

SOCIAL CHANGE IN LATIN AMERICA TODAY: Its Implications for United States Policy, by Richard N. Adams, John P. Gillin, Allan R. Holmberg, Oscar Lewis, Richard W. Patch, and Charles W. Wagley.

FOREIGN POLICY: THE NEXT PHASE: The 1960s (Revised Edition), by Thomas K. Finletter.

DEFENSE OF THE MIDDLE EAST: Problems of American Policy (Revised Edition), by John C. Campbell.

COMMUNIST CHINA AND ASIA: Challenge to American Policy, by A. Doak Barnett.

FRANCE, TROUBLED ALLY: De Gaulle's Heritage and Prospects, by Edgar S. Furniss, Jr.

THE SCHUMAN PLAN: A Study in Economic Cooperation, 1950-1959, by William Diebold, Jr.

SOVIET ECONOMIC AID: The New Aid and Trade Policy in Underdeveloped Countries, by Joseph S. Berliner.

RAW MATERIALS: A Study of American Policy, by Percy W. Bidwell.

NATO AND THE FUTURE OF EUROPE, by Ben T. Moore.

AFRICAN ECONOMIC DEVELOPMENT, by William A. Hance.

INDIA AND AMERICA: A Study of Their Relations, by Phillips Talbot and S. L. Poplai.

JAPAN BETWEEN EAST AND WEST, by Hugh Borton, Jerome B. Cohen, William J. Jorden, Donald Keene, Paul F. Langer and C. Martin Wilbur.

NUCLEAR WEAPONS AND FOREIGN POLICY, by Henry A. Kissinger.

MOSCOW-PEKING AXIS: Strengths and Strains, by Howard L. Boorman, Alexander Eckstein, Philip E. Mosely and Benjamin Schwartz.

CLIMATE AND ECONOMIC DEVELOPMENT IN THE TROPICS, by Douglas H. K. Lee.

WHAT THE TARIFF MEANS TO AMERICAN INDUSTRIES, by Percy W. Bidwell.

UNITED STATES SHIPPING POLICY, by Wytze Gorter.

RUSSIA AND AMERICA: Dangers and Prospects, by Henry L. Roberts.

STERLING: Its Meaning in World Finance, by Judd Polk.

FOREIGN AFFAIRS BIBLIOGRAPHY, 1942-1952, by Henry L. Roberts.

AMERICAN AGENCIES INTERESTED IN INTERNATIONAL AFFAIRS, compiled by Ruth Savord and Donald Wasson.

JAPANESE AND AMERICANS: A Century of Cultural Relations, by Robert S. Schwantes.